DRONES

WHAT EVERYONE NEEDS TO KNOW®

DRONES

WHAT EVERYONE NEEDS TO KNOW®

SARAH KREPS
Cornell University

OXFORD

UNIVERSITY PRESS

Oxford University Press is a department of the University of Oxford. It furthers
the University's objective of excellence in research, scholarship, and education
by publishing worldwide. Oxford is a registered trade mark of Oxford University
Press in the UK and certain other countries.

"What Everyone Needs to Know" is a registered
trademark of Oxford University Press.

Published in the United States of America by Oxford University Press
198 Madison Avenue, New York, NY 10016, United States of America.

© Oxford University Press 2016

First Edition published in 2016

Library of Congress Cataloging-in-Publication Data
Names: Kreps, Sarah E. (Sarah Elizabeth), author.
Title: Drones : what everyone needs to know / Sarah Kreps.
Description: New York, NY : Oxford University Press, [2016]
Identifiers: LCCN 2015040590| ISBN 978–0–19–023534–5 (hardcover: alk. paper) |
ISBN 978–0–19–023535–2 (pbk.: alk. paper)
Subjects: LCSH: Drone aircraft. | Air warfare.
Classification: LCC UG1242.D7 K73 2016 | DDC 623.74/69—dc23 LC record
available at http://lccn.loc.gov/2015040590

1 3 5 7 9 8 6 4 2
Printed by Courier Press, USA

CONTENTS

FOREWORD

My first encounter with the idea of a drone came in the days after the 9/11 terrorist attacks. I was a lieutenant in the E-3 Airborne Warning and Control System (AWACS) office outside Boston and worked on advanced programs related to the E-3 and other intelligence, surveillance, and reconnaissance systems. I recall my boss telling me that our office had received a "snowflake" originating with the Pentagon. Then-Secretary of Defense Donald Rumsfeld was famous for issuing snowflakes, a system of communication between the Secretary and the many employees of DoD. This particular snowflake was essentially an all-hands-on-deck call for our community to think through ways to retrofit as many Predators as possible with Hellfire missiles. Predators had been used for surveillance in the Balkans, but there had been reservations about arming them with missiles. After 9/11, the "gloves came off" and there was no question about whether the military would now make the decision to arm Predators. The question was how to do it quickly so they could be deployed to the field. The acquisitions community, of which I was a member, was not known for expediency. The Secretary, who was known for urging a leaner and meaner system, was trying to speed things up. He succeeded. The rest of the story is somewhat familiar. The Air Force, along with the CIA, deployed Predators to who reportedly survived the strike, in October 2001, with the first strike likely a CIA strike of the Taliban's number-three leader, Mullah Akhund, on November 8, 2001.[1]

After that initial introduction to unmanned aerial vehicles, often referred to as drones, I did not follow their employment much until 2011. By then I was a professor at Cornell University, having left the Air Force in 2003 to pursue a PhD that focused on issues of international security and defense policy. By that point, the wartime use of drones had not only spilled over into non-battlefield settings such as Pakistan, Somalia, and Yemen but had also escalated considerably. A US counterterrorism official reported that there had been about 305 drone strikes just in Pakistan between 2004 and 2011, with an estimated 2,050 individuals killed, of whom about 392 were civilians.

As a former military officer-turned political scientist, I could see the operational arguments in favor of drones but was concerned about the strategic and political ramifications. Drones, armed with precision weapons and able to loiter over targets, might actually be better positioned to minimize unintentional damage than alternatives such as local Pakistani air forces, for example, or ground troops. But because they imposed no risk to the country that used them, they could also create a moral hazard, being used in ways, times, and places that might not otherwise be used were these actors to use the caution that goes along with having skin in the game with manned aircraft or ground troops. Plus, from studying theories of democratic checks in wartime, I had a hunch that the populace, which would see few obvious burdens of a technology that introduced no casualties, would not be itching to end conflicts in which drones were involved. This could mean wars without limits in time or space.

I set out to study the politics, law, and ethics of drones. My first foray was with John Kaag, a colleague who studies philosophy. We wrote an academic article, several op-eds, and a book on the topic. The topic of drones did not seem to be going anywhere and I continued several other projects involving public opinion and drones. It turns out Americans think they love drones but it is in part because of how strikes and casualties are portrayed in media accounts, focusing on contentious assumptions such as the targets being militants rather than the possibility that these targets are civilians. Once individuals know of the possibility of civilian casualties, they are much more reticent in their support.

In 2013–2014, I was a resident fellow at the Council on Foreign Relations, where I turned to more policy-oriented questions. In particular, as a Stanton Nuclear Security Fellow, I was interested in drone proliferation, which is governed by the Missile Technology Control Regime (MTCR), the 1986 agreement that guided potential nuclear delivery vehicles, including drones. My colleague Micah Zenko and I worked on several articles for both *Foreign Affairs* and *Foreign Policy* as well as a Council Special Report, *Limiting Armed Drone Proliferation*. I then had the pleasure of hosting several Council on Foreign Relations roundtables on the topic everywhere from Dallas to Boston to New York to Tokyo, where I had the benefit of hearing a range of feedback on the topic.

It was around this time that Dave McBride, whom I had worked with on my first book, *Coalitions of Convenience*, approached me about writing the *Drones: What Everyone Needs to Know* book. He is a wonderful person to work with so I was tempted. Plus, it seemed like it was something I could write in my sleep after working on the topic for years. Wrong. The topic of drones is a moving target. It has evolved considerably in the last several years, as it surely will in the coming years. But it is endlessly fascinating and I hope the readers of this book agree.

In my writing of the book, I must obviously thank Dave for giving me the opportunity to write it, and to the various CFR Roundtables where I received feedback on the topic of drones. I would also like to thank Amy Zegart for inviting me to present my research at Stanford's Center for International Security and Cooperation and again as a Summer Security fellow at the Hoover Institution. I would also like to thank Frank Gavin for the invitation to present at the LBJ School of Government at UT-Austin and John Mearsheimer and Robert Pape for the opportunity to present at the University of Chicago's Program on International Security Policy.

I would also like to thank many individuals who collaborated on work related to this book, including John Kaag, Geoff Wallace, and Micah Zenko, as well as Neil Chitrao, Christian Covington, Shaan Franchi, and Jesse Saldana for valuable assistance in researching and editing the manuscript. As ever, I thank my family for being endlessly patient and supportive.

DRONES

WHAT EVERYONE NEEDS TO KNOW®

1

INTRODUCTION

Not a day goes by without another spectacular story about unmanned aerial vehicles (UAVs), also known as drones: Amazon announces it will deliver packages via drones, the US Federal Aviation Administration (FAA) worries that drones given as holiday gifts will become safety hazards as they take to the skies, the New Zealand government releases a request for proposals to use drones to combat pests and disease on the ground, and Google renames itself Alphabet, whose marquee innovation is its future drone delivery service. These stories have a way of captivating the mind. They bring together the world of science fiction and 21st-century consumer culture that values instant gratification and personalized service. Yet the commonplace, and now barely newsworthy, stories remain about American drones killing suspected militants in Pakistan.

Drones, both for the civilian and military applications, are clearly here to stay. The aerospace analyst Teal Group projects that spending on unmanned systems and sensors will increase 73% in the next decade, totaling $89 billion.[1] Much of that increase is on the military side, where the United States but increasingly also other countries are investing in drones. Drones are also in high demand by civilians with both recreational and commercial interests. By some estimates, the number of drones in US airspace could reach 30,000 by 2020.[2] Those drones will operate in the service of law enforcement, border patrol, real estate photography, crop inspections, and other tasks that are too "dirty, dull, or dangerous" for humans yet well-suited to drones.

The increased use of drones raises a number of questions and concerns. First, how does the proliferation of military drones both within and across countries affect international and regional security? President Obama acknowledged in 2013 that being able to deploy drones with little scrutiny or risk caused him to see drones as a "cure-all" for terrorism, with the United States using drones more often than it would alternatives such as manned aircraft or ground troops. This tendency to rely on drones at times and in ways that actors would not otherwise use force has enormous and troublesome implications if replicated in countries that acquire armed drones in the future, in other words, each of these countries could come to see drones as the cure-all to their domestic or regional security challenges. This is especially true in regions such as East Asia and the Middle East, which are already susceptible to conflict. The proliferation of armed drones also has potentially destabilizing consequences in a domestic context where states might be more inclined to use drones as a low-risk option against insurgents, for example in China, Turkey, or Russia.

Second, can the use of nonmilitary drones including for recreational purposes increase without compromising safety? The FAA reports about 25 incidents per month in which drones have flown too close to manned aircraft or airports.[3] There have been a number of well-publicized incidents involving hobbyist drones meddling with wildfire prevention efforts, flying around major sporting events, or landing near heads of state. Federal regulations may seek to limit such activities in part by requiring that individuals register their drones, or companies themselves may try to limit where individuals can fly drones through "geofencing" software, but enforcement promises to be a challenge.

Third, does the increased use of drones raise potential privacy concerns? Americans express reservations related to recreational use of drones but especially about the use of drones for law enforcement. As of 2013, 30 states had initiated legislation against drones. As one state senator in Virginia argued, "I think it's important to get ahead on issues like these before they get out of control ... we can imagine the problems that drones will bring in the future." He proposed a bill that would put a moratorium on drones because of potential violations of the Fourth Amendment of the Constitution, the right against "unlawful search and seizure." It was the first anti-drone legislation passed in the country.[4]

Cities and countries have followed suit. Seattle's Police Department had acquired two drones only to have them decommissioned and transferred to the Los Angeles Police Department (LAPD) without having been used. The LAPD, in turn, then faced public outcry over the question of how the drones would be used and put a moratorium on their use. Some countries have outlawed domestic drones altogether. The FAA still bans commercial drones in national airspace, though it has granted more than a number of exemptions and is reviewing hundreds more as of the end of 2014. This pattern in itself creates the prospect of writing policy through a series of exemptions, which would reflect a certain ad hocness rather than purposeful design.

In order to understand the implications of drones as their uses change, the book begins by looking at their roots in military use. It then surveys commercial use and the regulation of drones both domestically and internationally. As Chris Anderson, the former editor-in-chief of *Wired* magazine, describes drones in the context of agriculture, "what started as a military technology may end up better known as a green-tech tool, and our kids will grow up used to flying robots buzzing over farms like tiny crop dusters."[5] While commercial applications seem to be growing, they still represent only a small percentage of the market, about 11% of that spending, compared to 89% of the spending on military drones. While the proportion of investment in civilian drones is expected to reach 14% within a decade, it is still a small fraction compared to that spent on military drones.[6]

Consistent with the investment of resources over time, the book focuses its analysis on the military use of drones. However, it also looks into the burgeoning uses of drones for civilian purposes, including individual industries and the turn to recreational use. During the 2014 holiday season, "drone" joined "house," "car," and "stock" in populating the top of Google's auto-fill list when someone typed, "I want to buy." Or as *The Verge* put it, "there's no cooler toy right now than a drone."[7] For as little as $100, individuals can increasingly buy small drones such as the mini-drone made by Parrot, a French company whose sales have increased 300% per year since 2012. While recreational drones flown in the United States are still required to fly within the line of sight and no higher than 400 ft., they are increasingly popular as "the functional descendent of the thoroughly nerdy RC plane; [with] an injection of edginess due to their big brothers' militaristic misdeeds."[8] The same is true abroad. Even the Pope now has a yellow and white drone, the colors of the Vatican flag, with the papal emblem emblazoned on it. As the school that gave Pope Francis the drone noted in a statement, the drone represents "the values of technology in the service of man," noting the helpful applications for earthquake relief after the big Nepal earthquake.[9]

With the increased demand for drones has come increased attentiveness toward their regulation. The question of how to regulate drones is a nettlesome one, given the vast range of applications, both recreational and commercial, and the growing volume of each. But the status quo is also problematic, as made manifest by the January 2015 incident in which a hobby drone, operated by an inebriated government worker, landed on the lawn of the White House. Against this backdrop, it is not surprising that the new world of drones has been referred to as the "wild west" when it comes to regulations on their use, referring to the growing number of such incidents, uncertainty about how to balance safety with the seemingly inevitable spread of drones, and ability to enforce any existing and future legislation.[10]

Beyond starting with military drones and turning to commercial drones later in the book, the book largely focuses its lens on the United States before turning to other countries. Although Israel helped initiate and deploy many of the unmanned military technologies in the 1980s, it has been the United States that has represented more than half of the world's research and development and procurement costs until now, according to the Teal Group's forecast. The United States accounts for 62% of worldwide spending on research and development and 55% of procurement. As the Congressional Research Service concludes, "the Department of Defense Remains the Key Driver" of drones because of its development and acquisitions related to the wars in Iraq, Afghanistan, "and other countries where terrorist groups were or are active."[11] This dominance is projected to change in the coming years as the rest of the world increases its spending, especially in procurement, but the United States and in particular the United States *military* represent a useful starting point in terms of understanding drones in general.[12]

Nonetheless, the next chapter in the story about drones is about proliferation to countries other than the United States. Between 2005 and 2011, the number of countries with drones went from 41 to 76. The increase consisted primarily of tactical drones that have limited range and are nonlethal, but a number of countries have observed the US experience with combat drones and sought to acquire them as well. As President Obama himself acknowledged in a major speech about drones in May 2013, "the very precision of drone strikes and the necessary secrecy often involved in such actions can end up shielding our government from the public scrutiny that a troop deployment invites."[13] The ability to use force at no risk to one's own troops while skirting domestic criticism is clearly attractive to states, evidenced by the growing proliferation of armed drones. Russia reports that its development of a combat UAV, which it plans to begin testing in 2017, is meant to emulate the US drones that have conducted strikes in places such as Afghanistan and Pakistan. Russia now has a base near Moscow dedicated to the training of drone operators.[14] Israel and the United Kingdom have already used drones in combat; Iran and China are thought to have armed drones; and others such as Pakistan, India, Turkey, and the United Arab Emirates are trying to acquire armed drones as well.

Lastly, the book focuses most on aerial systems as opposed to unmanned sea and ground vehicles. Almost all of the development having to do with drones has taken place on the aerial side. In the United States military, for example, more than 90% of the research and development and procurement has been allocated for aerial systems, and that trend is projected to continue into the foreseeable future. In 2014, air systems funding amounted to $3.8 billion compared to just $13 million for ground and $330 million for maritime, with air making up the lion's share of the $4.12 billion total. The trends are consistently tilted toward aerial systems through 2018.[15] While ground and maritime systems receive treatment later in the book, the aerial drone is its primary focus.

In short, the book covers quite a bit of territory, but a survey of every country, every technology, and every modality is beyond its reach. Nonetheless, it seeks to highlight the most prominent developments of the past, while looking at likely or promising developments in the future. While that journey is sometimes technical, as it travels from avionics to political science, its other aim is to reach an audience that reads the news headlines about drones on a daily basis and wants to learn more.

2

ARMED DRONE TECHNOLOGY

Over the last decade, the United States went from having unarmed surveillance drones to sophisticated armed drones capable of conducting prolonged surveillance and then killing the target. This chapter will take stock of those developments by answering a number of questions that provide context for the recent evolution of armed drone technology.

Q. What is a drone?

The term "drone" has come to loosely refer to "unmanned aerial vehicles" (UAVs), or what the Federal Aviation Administration (FAA) refers to as an "unmanned aerial system" (UAS) and the US Air Force to as a "remotely piloted aircraft" (RPA). The latter organization prefers to incorporate "pilot" because of the significant training required, even for a remotely positioned operator. All of these names speak to the attribute that unifies drones: that they operate without pilots on-board.

For some observers, this essentially means that everything is a drone. As Kelsey Atherton of *Popular Science* puts it, " 'drone' as a category refers to any unmanned, remotely piloted flying craft, ranging from something as small as a radio-controlled toy helicopter to the 32,000-lb., $104 million Global Hawk. If it flies and it's controlled by a pilot on the ground, it fits under the everyday-language definition of drone."[1] Despite this broad definition, Atherton suggests that until recently, model airplanes have been governed by a different set of laws from drones. Indeed, Canadian laws have distinguished between drones and hobby aircraft, stating that a drone is "a power-driven aircraft, other than a model aircraft, that is designed to fly without a human operator on board."[2] For the United States, the line between drones and model aircraft is increasingly blurred. In 2015, the FAA passed regulations requiring any unmanned aircraft greater than 0.55 pound and less than 55 pounds to register their aircraft (those greater than 55 pounds require FAA approval, a step beyond registration), which effectively includes model aircraft. All unmanned aerial systems (UAS), as the FAA calls them, must fly below 400 feet, be kept within the visual line of sight, and not fly within 5 miles of an airport.

Indeed, one reason the FAA essentially subsumed model aircraft is that the line between the two is increasingly arbitrary as drones have become smaller and hobbyist model aircraft have become more sophisticated. For example, hobby aircraft can be equipped with first-person view (FPV) capabilities in which a camera is mounted in front of the model aircraft and flying the aircraft via a video down-link that is displayed on either a portable monitor or video goggles, thus extending the visual range of the pilot and raising concerns about collisions. At the point that this FPV goes beyond the line of sight, the FAA would likely consider it a drone that would fall under their regulatory framework. However, operating within the line of sight does not mean an aircraft is *not* a drone. Quadcopters are traditionally operated within the line of sight and yet they are commonly considered drones.

Another source of potential confusion is the difference between a drone and cruise missile. While the Missile Technology Control Regime (MTCR, which will be discussed later) considers cruise missiles as a type of drone, they are actually distinct platforms. As with drones and model aircraft, cruise missiles can be confused with drones because they too are unmanned. However, drones, according to the Defense Department, are meant to be recovered while cruise missiles are one-way systems. Furthermore, a cruise missile's munitions are integrated into its airframe, while the drone's are more segregated and detached.[3] In addition, while both drones and cruise missiles are used for stand-off strikes, drones have a shorter range and are slower than cruise missiles. The one-way nature of cruise missiles, their long-range capability, and their speed as compared to drones impacts the types of missions for which cruise missiles and drones are used. Drones are therefore more likely to require forward operating bases because of their limited range compared to cruise missiles.[4]

Even this theoretical difference between drones and cruise missiles can become blurred by some of the drones operated by countries other than the United States. For example, Israel has developed a weapons system that is considered a drone (the Harop, also known as the Harpy) that is essentially a one-way drone in which the platform itself acts as the munition, though it does carry limited amounts (less than 10 kg or less than 5 lb.) of explosives in its nose. In this regard, the drone is essentially acting as something of a suicide aircraft, rocket, or cruise missile. What makes this drone different from a cruise missile is its ability to loiter over a target; after loitering, it attacks by self-destructing into the target.

Q. What is the historical genealogy of armed drones?

Identifying the first appearance of drones in warfare depends on the definition of drone being used, which the previous discussion suggests can present a vexing question. If one considers a drone simply to be a remotely piloted vehicle, then one could say that the first balloons used in battle were drones. Indeed, using this definition, which would require some conceptual stretching, the first occurrence of drones occurred in 1849, when Austria attacked Venice with nearly 200 explosive-laden unmanned balloons. Once the balloons were over Venice, the explosives were detonated "by means of a long isolated copper wire with a large galvanic battery."[5] While the Austrian attack helped lay the groundwork for the use of drones in war, the operation was far from a glowing success—some of the balloons were blown back over Austrian lines. Moreover, these vehicles were remotely piloted only insofar as they depended on the direction of the wind.

World War I saw the testing and development of another set of remotely piloted vehicles, though none actually operated before the war ended. One such vehicle developed by Orville Wright and Charles Kettering during WWI, but not used in battle, was the Kettering Bug; it was a 12-foot-long wooden biplane weighing only 530 lb. (including a 180-lb. bomb). To get the Kettering Bug to fly the right distance, operators had to account for wind speed and direction, and then calculate the correct number of engine revolutions required; then, the vehicle would act as an unmanned torpedo that would strike a target. The Dayton-Wright Airplane Company built around 50 of the unmanned vehicles, though this system acted more as the Harop discussed above, rather than what we would think of as the two-way Predator or Reaper.

Between WWI and WWII, the United Kingdom and the United States both developed a series of radio-controlled drones which they used primarily as aerial targets on which their pilots could practice. In the 1930s, the Royal Air Force began developing the de Havilland Tiger Moth, a training aircraft used for target practice. In 1935, a variant of the Tiger Moth came online called the Queen Bee, thought to be the namesake for the term "drone" often used to describe unmanned systems because the rear cockpit had a radio-control system. The Queen Bee had a radio-control system in the rear cockpit that allowed the aircraft to be flown unmanned and under radio control, which was of course desirable given its role as a target drone for anti-aircraft gunnery practice. While the company made 400 of these aircraft, almost all were destroyed, having served the function for which it was intended.

Around the same time, Reginald Denny, an actor and former member of the British Royal Flying Corps, formed a model plane shop that eventually became the Radioplane Company—which was later acquired by Northrop Grumman. The Radioplane Company developed inexpensive radio-controlled aircraft that could be used for training antiaircraft gunners, similar to the purpose of the Queen Bee. The company's most popular aircraft was the OQ-3 target drone, with over 9,000 manufactured for the US Army during WWII. It is this aircraft that Norma Jeane, who later became known as Marilyn Monroe, helped assemble during the war. She was spotted by an Army photographer in June 1945, photographed, and, as a veteran of drone-building in World War II, became a model soon after the war's end.

During WWII, both Germany and the United States began developing more sophisticated unmanned platforms. At the beginning of WWII, Adolf Hitler commissioned a project to develop an unmanned vehicle used in combat, which resulted in the V-1 rocket, which was more like an early cruise missile than drone, although it was later used as a target drone by the French after the V-1 technology fell into their hands toward the end of the war. The V-1 had a range of approximately 160 miles, permitting the Germans to use launch sites in France to hit targets across the Channel. The weapon killed over 900 British citizens and injured over 35,000 in Britain during WWII. To counter the V-1, the US Navy developed drones that were able to destroy the launch sites. These drones took off with a two-person crew that would bail after setting a course for the target. The vehicles were then flown by remote control and were often successful in eliminating the ramps the Germans used to launch the V-1s.

In the postwar period, the United States continued in the target drone business, developing a series of Firebee aircraft that could be launched from the air or the ground. The subsequent generations of Firebees made slight modifications on this principle until the contractor produced a reconnaissance version, called the Lightning Bug, which was used extensively in Vietnam. Toward the end of the Vietnam War the

United States transferred 33 Lightning Bugs to Israel to be used in their 1973 Yom Kippur War.

As drone analyst, Chris Cole puts it, the more contemporary drones were "the offspring not of the American initiatives of the 1960s but of the Israeli initiatives of the 1980s."[6] In particular, the technology was used in the service of surveillance of troop movements, among other things, during the 1982 invasion of Lebanon.[7] During this time the Israelis, who remain one of the two largest producers of drones, began building several surveillance drones—including several that were sold to the United States. The Pioneer, for example, was used in the 1991 Gulf War. Israeli Abraham Karem also developed the Gnat, which he later sold to General Atomics. The company used the design as the archetype for its Predator. The United States deployed the Gnat 750 for surveillance in the early 1990s in Yugoslavia, followed by the unarmed Predator during the conflict in Bosnia and Kosovo. The Predator improved upon the Gnat 750 with more accurate targeting technology using advanced sensors.

Like previous drones, the Predator remained unarmed. The US Air Force discussed the possibility of arming the aircraft and investigated whether or not an armed Predator would be compliant with the Intermediate-range Nuclear Forces (INF) Treaty. The INF treaty bans warheads from a "self-propelled vehicle that sustains flight through the use of aerodynamic lift over most of its flight," specifically "a ground-launched cruise missile that is a weapon-delivery vehicle."[8] In their legal deliberations, the Air Force, in consultation with the State Department, determined that an armed drone was outside this ban and that an armed drone would not violate the treaty.[9] Nonetheless, while General Atomics had equipped a Predator with a Hellfire missile and successfully fired it in a February 2001 practice flight, the decision to field armed Predators had languished until the 9/11 attacks. "It was the War on Terror that finally enabled the military to weaponize drones, giving them the capability to take out designated targets."[10] Armed drones became a way to expand the range of options but without risks to American personnel.

The Predator deployed to Afghanistan soon after the 9/11 attacks, and by November 2001, the CIA had conducted about 40 Hellfire missile strikes in Afghanistan. In comparison to the number of airstrikes by manned platforms, which numbered 6,500 in the first three months of the war, the reliance on drone strikes was still minimal, though the scope of operations soon expanded to places other than Afghanistan. In 2002, the first drone strike outside an active combat zone occurred in Yemen. The CIA used a Predator to target Ali Qaed Senyan Al-Harthi, who was linked to the bombing of the USS *Cole* in 2000, as well as several individuals suspected of being Al-Qaeda affiliates.

What followed was a roughly two-year pause in drone strikes for counterterrorism—that is, the strikes against sus-pected terrorists carried out outside active battlefields such as Afghanistan or Iraq—until the United States expanded such strikes into Pakistan in 2004. It conducted the first such strike against a suspected Al-Qaeda facilitator, Nek Muhammad, and four other suspected militants, beginning a long and increas-ingly sharp increase of drone strikes in Pakistan. While the United States conducted 52 strikes in Pakistan between 2001 and 2008, there were 300 in the four years following (2009–2012), a steep escalation in counterterrorist drone strikes that made the United States the leading state in the use of armed drones.[11] During this time, drone strikes in conflict zones also increased, with the British increasingly complementing US attacks in Afghanistan, allegedly accounting for about one-fifth of drone strikes by 2012.[12] Thus, in a somewhat dramatic fashion, the use of drones after the 9/11 terrorist attacks quickly revealed the potentially transformative nature of armed drones both in active conflict zones and in the context of counterterrorism.

Q. What types of drones are or will be available?

As mentioned above, the attribute that unifies drones is that they are all remotely piloted. Beyond those similarities, the differences are vast. They vary enormously in terms of size, capability, and range. Some are semiautonomous, meaning they rely on a human in some fashion—even if remotely. Others are autonomous, in which case the system is preprogrammed and based on the artificial intelligence of the robot making decisions. Some are armed; others are used for intelligence, surveillance, and reconnaissance. Some are hand-launched; others can take off and land by themselves from an airfield. Given the large range of aircraft that can plausibly fit under the heading of drones, it is not surprising that there are many ways to categorize them.

The main international institution that regulates drones is the MTCR, a 1987 regime that sought to limit proliferation of nuclear delivery vehicles, including drones. Drones with a payload of over 1,102 lb. and a range of 186 miles or greater were classified as Category I systems. This includes Global Hawk drones, which are only used for reconnaissance and surveillance, and armed Predators and Reapers, which have been used in combat in Afghanistan, Pakistan, and Somalia, among other countries, and are seen as being more capacious and therefore only able to be licensed for export on rare occasions. Category II systems include materials that are less sensitive but still capable of covering a range of 186 miles, irrespective of payload, and have less stringent export prohibitions. An example includes Iran's Ababil, a reconnaissance, surveillance, and attack aircraft that has a payload of 40 kg (or about 88 lb.) and is thought to be the system exported to Hezbollah and potentially Venezuela.[13] Some drones fall outside the MTCR altogether—meaning they can be exported without any scrutiny—and these include smaller-scale, limited-range drones, or smaller drones that are designed for one-way missions.

While the MTCR classification focuses primarily on payload and range, a related categorization is to organize by capacity, an aggregation of dimensions such as altitude, range, and endurance, which tends to correlate with the type of mission or operation that the drone could carry out. These categories include mini, tactical, and strategic drones, depicted in Table 2.1 and drawn from the 2012 Government Accountability Office report on drone proliferation.[14]

Table 2.1 Categories of Drones Organized by a Combination of Altitude, Range, and Endurance

Category	Mini	Tactical	Strategic
Attitude	Low	Low to medium	Medium to high
Endurance	Short (about an hour)	Medium (up to several hours)	Long (ranges from hours to days)
Range	Close-range	Limited to line-of-sight (approximately 300 kilometers or less) (about 186 miles)	Long range
Example	Raven	Shadow	Global Hawk

Source: CIA (information); DOD (photos).

Nonproliferation: Agencies Could Improve Information Sharing and End-Use Monitoring on Unmanned Aerial Vehicle Exports. United States Government Accountability Office, July 2012

Mini-drones are designed for quick deployment and easy mobility, making them ideal for reconnaissance, surveillance, and target acquisition. These drones include the Raven, which the manufacturer (AeroVironment) reported in 2015 is "the most widely used unmanned aircraft system in the world today." These systems are launched by hand and powered by an electric motor, and have the capability to be operated remotely or operated autonomously using global positioning system (GPS) navigation. Because they do not require intricate support systems, mini-drones are ideal for supporting forward-deployed units within the army.

Tactical drones are designed for reconnaissance, battle damage assessment, surveillance, and target acquisition; they are launched from a pneumatic catapult mounted on a trailer and recovered with equipment meant to decelerate the drone as it lands. One of the most common examples of the tactical drone is the Shadow, which the US military had planned to weaponize contingent on having sufficient funds.[15]

Strategic drones are used for many of the same purposes as tactical drones but are able to fly higher, farther, and for longer periods of time. Strategic drones include the Global Hawk, the Predator B, and its successor, the Reaper, which has a large number of functions including reconnaissance, surveillance, weapons delivery, and targeting, and can fly for over 30 hours without refueling.

The Rand Corporation has yet another classification system, organizing drones into four categories based on a two-by-two matrix describing whether the technology is long or short range and high or low technology: (1) long-range, high-technology such as the Predator or Reaper; (2) long-range, low-technology such as the Iranian Ababil; (3) short-range, high-technology such as the Raven; and (4) short-range, low-technology such as model airplanes.[16]

Another way to think of the differences across drones would be based on function. The typologies above tend to group nonlethal and lethal drones together; for example, the

Global Hawk and Reaper would both be considered strategic or Category I drones. Treating these two types of drones in the same category is potentially misguided given the quite different uses of each: the Global Hawk is used for reconnaissance and the Reaper for killing terrorists. A classification that would address the broad, different uses might instead consider drones used in the service of surveillance and reconnaissance (not directly lethal) and those that are equipped with weapons and used directly for lethal purposes, while also taking into account range. Other typologies have therefore built on this distinction between lethal and nonlethal drones, classifying drones into 1) tactical drones that are smaller-scale drones such has the Raven and Shadow; 2) advanced, unarmed drones such as the Global Hawk; and 3) advanced, armed drones such as the Predator and Reaper.[17]

The various typologies of drones are useful because they put the threat of drones and drone proliferation into context. For example, the General Accountability Office released a report in 2012 showing that 76 countries had acquired drones by 2011, compared to just 41 in 2005; the conclusion one should not reach is that these are all armed Reapers capable of eliminating terrorists at long range.[18] Rather, most of these countries make it onto the GAO's list simply because they have tactical drones that have limited range and nonlethal capability that would present few regional security consequences. Only a handful of countries have lethal strategic drones. This helps put the potential threat of drones into perspective, making it less consequential than it might initially seem on its face.

Moreover, since few of those 76 countries have advanced armed drones, it puts the proliferation challenge in perspective. If all of these countries had already acquired advanced armed drones, then it would make little sense to have a restrictive set of transfer or export policies. But the fact that the most advanced armed drones have been out of reach for most countries suggests considerable merit to a system that keeps close hold at least over the types of armed drones that do pose threats to international and regional security. Those proliferation questions receive careful treatment later in the book.

Q. Who has used armed drones in combat, and where have they been used?

As of 2015, Israel, the United Kingdom, the United States, Pakistan, and Hezbollah all used armed drones in combat, although the first three countries have been the most prolific users and are the focus of this section. Israel has used armed drones both in the Gaza war and in Sinai. Israel's early use of drones came in the 1970s, when they were used for surveillance for the 1973 Yom Kippur War and later in 1982 to locate targets in the First Lebanon War. Though the evidence is thin, due to the highly secretive nature of the Israeli program, Israel likely first used armed drones in 2004. *The Jerusalem Post* claimed that a "pilotless aircraft" had been used to strike targets in Gaza. Later that year it appeared that Israel used a drone to target a suspected Palestinian jihadist militant. During the 2006 Lebanon War drones were likely used, as they probably also were in late 2006 during an American military strike targeting Gaza. Palestinian sources suggest that Israel again sent armed drones to strike targets in Gaza in 2007, and most notably in 2008–2009, during Operation Cast Lead, during which about a dozen drones were airborne at all times.[19] One Palestinian rights group claims that during this conflict Israel conducted 42 drone strikes, killing 87 civilians. The Israeli Air Force again used armed drones in its 2012 Gaza conflict, Operation Pillar of Defense, with an estimated 24 civilians killed.[20] Israel has also used drones in isolated cases in Sinai, targeting militants suspected of trafficking in weapons from Egypt.[21]

The United Kingdom has conducted a number of drone strikes in Afghanistan using its US-made Reapers, though the last crew appears to have left Afghanistan in November 2014. Between 2008 and 2014, the British Reapers conducted almost 5,000 Reaper sorties, firing more than 450 missiles during that time. Although its last crew had left Afghanistan, UK drone operations in Syria and Iraq were increasing, with a number of Reapers having been sent to the region. Between January and June 2015, the United Kingdom had conducted 350 Reaper missions in Iraq, and 107 in Syria, though the strikes appear to be restricted to Iraq, which saw 97 actual strikes during that time period.[22]

By far, the United States has been the most frequent user of armed drones. These strikes can be organized around strikes in active battle zones such as Afghanistan, Iraq, and Libya, which constitute the largest percentage of strikes. The first recorded use of an armed drone by any country took place in November 2001, with a Predator striking a target in Afghanistan. In recent years, the data on strikes in Afghanistan has become classified, making it impossible to update the trends, though between 2008 and 2012 it appears as though there were almost 1,000 strikes in Afghanistan. Another 105 strikes occurred in the 2011 Yemen conflict, and several others took place in the earlier phase of the Iraq War.

More recently, a coalition involving the United States and the United Kingdom struck targets in both Iraq and Syria, with the intention of eliminating the Islamic State of Iraq and Syria (ISIS) strongholds. Data from *Reuters* reveals that whereas the United States had carried about 37% of coalition strikes in the first three months of the campaign from September to November, by December 2014 it had reached about 97% of strikes.[23] About 15% were drone strikes,[24] although the rates appear to fluctuate and drones have carried out a number of high-profile attacks, including the one in August 2015 that killed Junaid Hussain, a senior ISIS recruiter, propagandist, and cyberspecialist.

Beyond these strikes in active conflict zones, the United States has conducted hundreds of counterterrorism strikes in Pakistan, Yemen, and Somalia. While the United States does not report details on these strikes, and generally does not acknowledge them at all, particularly those conducted by the CIA, advocacy groups have expended considerable resources trying to uncover the details of covert strikes. The Bureau of

Investigative Journalism (BIJ), the New America Foundation (NAM), and *The Long War Journal* have all collected data on the number of strikes, and Amnesty International, Human Rights Watch, and Stanford/NYU Law have added case-specific details to this data, doing on-site interviews with relatives and friends of drone strike victims. The reporting that these organizations have done serves as a relatively credible source of strikes in nonactive battlefield zones. As Table 2.2 shows, most of these strikes have taken place in Pakistan, with a peak of about 122 strikes in the year of 2010, but dozens of others scattered across more than a decade have taken place in Somalia and Yemen.

As the data shows, the rate of strikes has decreased since 2010. There are several potential reasons for the drop. One is that the strikes eliminated many of the high-value targets that were on the strike list. Another factor, not incompatible with the first, is that the United States became more careful with

Table 2.2 Estimates of the Number of Strikes per Country per Year, 2002–2014

Year	Pakistan	Yemen	Somalia
2002	0	1	0
2003	0	0	0
2004	1	0	0
2005	3	0	0
2006	2	0	0
2007	4	0	0
2008	36	0	0
2009	54	2	0
2010	122	4	0
2011	73	10	5
2012	48	54	2
2013	27	26	1
2014	24	14	2

Source: BIJ.

the strikes it did conduct. A number of former US officials have expressed concerns about whether the strikes were creating more terrorists than they were killing, that is to say, were working tactically but not strategically, and that the United States should raise the bar in terms of targets, only killing the most notable ones. When President Obama appeared to usher in a new policy on drones that would be more restrictive and transparent—a move some critics suggested was more about words than actions[25]—long-time observers such as the *New York Times'* Scott Shane attributed the shift to "a changing calculation of the long-term costs and benefits of targeted killings."[26] In other words, the administration had come to see drones as less valuable against the remaining targets, with the costs of such strikes mounting from a public relations standpoint. Nonetheless, the "tactic, once intended to be rare, has become completely routine," according to the Council on Foreign Relations' Micah Zenko, as he reflected on the 500th non-battlefield-targeted killing in November 2014.[27] In 2014 there were nearly as many drone strikes in Pakistan as the year before, 24 versus 27; there were somewhat fewer in Yemen than in the year before; and there was one more in Somalia than in the year before.

Q. How many fatalities have resulted from covert drone strikes?

The fatalities associated with these strikes are difficult to assess since different organizations have generated different estimates of militants and civilians killed. Based on the accounts of the three main groups which have collected the data—the NAF, *The Long War Journal*, and the BIJ—the total number of individuals killed has been close to 4,000 as of 2014. By some accounts, only about 2.5–5% of the targeted killing victims are militant leaders, with the vast majority being foot soldiers, and a smaller number being civilians.[28] Table 2.3 summarizes the fatality estimates of targeted killings in Pakistan, Yemen, and Somalia from 2002 to 2014.

Table 2.3 Estimates of the Total Number of Strikes per Country, 2002–2014

Country	Strikes	Total Killed	Civilians Killed	% Civilians
Pakistan	376	2924	376.5	13%
Yemen	88	635	87.5	15%
Somalia	17	114	28	24.7%

Source: Micah Zenko, "US Transparency and the Truth of Targeted Killings." CFR.org, September 5, 2014.

Table 2.4 Operations in 2014 in Pakistan, Yemen, and Somalia, Based on the BIJ's Data

Country	Strikes	Total Killed	Civilians Killed	% Civilians
Pakistan	22	104–168	0–2	~1%
Yemen	13–15	82–118	4–9	~5.5%
Somalia	2	8–15	0	0%

While the United States had held off on drone strikes in Pakistan in the first half of the year, granting Pakistan latitude to try negotiating a deal with the Taliban, the number picked up in the latter half, with about two dozen attacks during 2014. As Table 2.4 suggests, the percentage of civilians killed in the most recent year for which complete data was available (2014) is lower than the average between 2002 and 2014. Given these apparent shifts in the civilian casualty rate, advocacy groups have taken notice and investigated the casualty trends.

Indeed, the civilian casualty figures have proven to be quite controversial, as there tend to be discrepancies across studies. A meta-study—in other words, a study about studies—examining the casualty data from three major think tanks and the two nongovernmental organizations cited above identifies a large range of casualty estimates. Offering a more in-depth look at casualty differences across studies, Table 2.5 compares the numbers across these studies for just one country and one year: Pakistan 2011. It shows the wide variation in terms of estimated civilian casualties even while the overall

Table 2.5 Variation in Fatality Estimates across Studies for Strikes in Pakistan in 2011

Target	NAF	*Long War Journal*	BIJ[29]	CHRC
Militant	303–502	405	N/A	330–575
Civilian	57–65	30	52–146	72–155
Unknown	32–37	N/A	N/A	N/A
Total	392–604	435	447–660	456–661
Civilian Casualty Rate	**9–17%**	**7%**	**8–33%**	**11–34%**

totals are within the same ballpark, with one analysis in the single digits for civilian casualty rates and other entities as high as 33–34%.

The meta-study found that the biggest reason for discrepancies across studies is that each uses different designations for militant and civilian such that reading the same account of a strike victim, one group will check a box in the militant column while the other will use the civilian column, and still others will use the "unknown" column for potential ambiguity. The challenge is that the legal definition of combatant is ambiguous, defined as an individual directly participating in hostilities. As an illustration of how contentious this definition can be, in 2012 the *New York Times* created a stir by reporting that the Obama administration designates "all military-age males in a strike zone as combatants." Such an accounting system would certainly produce lower estimates of civilian deaths, which is why the administration's declaration that its strikes had produced zero civilian casualties in 2014 had raised eyebrows. Groups such as the BIJ refer to this practice as "false accounting" and designate many of these same "militants" as civilians. As one observer concluded, the range across and even within studies is "so large that it actually tells us very little about whether drone strikes are killing a great many or a small number of innocent people—or somewhere in between. In that sense, the best methodology only serves to demonstrate how little we actually know about the civilian casualties from U.S. drone strikes."[30]

While a number of groups have worked to create transparency in terms of overall drone strikes, going for breadth in their analysis, other groups have carried out more focused studies within a particular country or year, aiming for depth. For example, Amnesty International investigated nine drone strikes in North Waziristan between January 2012 and August 2013; Human Rights Watch examined six drone strikes in Yemen during a period between 2009 and 2013; and the Columbia Law School's Human Rights Clinic (CHRC) studied Pakistani drone strikes in 2011. These all focus their attention on whether those individuals reported as militants were in fact culpable by conducting interviews on the ground, in the case of Amnesty and Human Rights Watch, and in the case of CHRC by using the data from the first three studies to arrive at their own conclusions about the number of drone strike casualties in Pakistan in 2011. Each of these focused studies seeks to expose the fact that the actual number of civilian fatalities was far more than not only government accounts but even those of media outlets, which are unable to field reporters in the dangerous regions where drone strikes occur.

At the least, the more focused examinations of civilian casualties have uncovered a number of deaths in episodes where the US government had stated that the strike had not produced any civilian casualties. In some cases, the strikes were "double-tap" strikes that killed rescuers who were coming in to claim the bodies originally targeted, another involved an assembly of elders, and a third struck six school children. Researchers also found that in these cases, drone strikes were actually more likely to kill innocent civilians than manned aircraft because the drone pilots were comparatively less proficient in their training on minimizing civilian harm.[31] The studies, which focused on a subset of strikes, may be vulnerable to the criticism that the particular strikes are not representative of strikes in general, and therefore could be flukes rather than an indication of policy. Nonetheless, human rights groups point out that even if these episodes are outliers, they are sufficiently egregious that they should raise flags in terms of the soundness of the policies. While far from the last word, the analyses also pose important questions about the credibility and transparency of the US government, which has not been forthcoming in reconciling the discrepancies in these accounts.

Q. What are the advantages of using drones in combat?

Several factors have made armed drones appear to be the "cure-all" for counterterrorism, as President Obama referred to the administration's reliance on drones. First, drones allow for sustained presence over potential targets. The existing US arsenal of armed drones—primarily the Predator and Reaper—can remain aloft, fully loaded with munitions, for over 14 hours, compared to four hours or less for F-16 fighter jets and A-10 ground attack aircraft. The SolarEagle, a solar-powered drone that Boeing and the Defense Advanced Research Projects Agency (DARPA) are developing, will be able to remain in the air for five years because of its efficient electronic motors and a long wingspan to maximize solar absorption. The advantages for loitering and persistence compared to aircraft are evident, but the operational duration of a drone flying at stratospheric altitudes offers a plausible replacement for satellites, which are costly and can present nettlesome aerospace engineering challenges.

Second, drones provide a near-instantaneous responsiveness —dramatically shrinking what US military targeting experts call the "find-fix-finish" loop—that most other platforms lack. For example, a drone loiters over targets, collecting intelligence in real-time for hours, days, and sometimes weeks. Then the drone-fired missile travels faster than the speed of sound, striking a target within seconds—often before it is heard by people on the ground. This ability stands in stark contrast to the August 1998 cruise missile salvo targeting Osama bin Laden, which had to be programmed based on projections of where he would be in four to six hours, in order to allow time to analyze the intelligence, obtain presidential authorization, program the missiles, and fly them to the target.

Third, and most important, unmanned systems do not face the limitations associated with manned systems. In particular, drones do not risk the death or capture of human pilots or ground forces since unlike manned aircraft or raids by soldiers, drones fly directly over hostile territory without placing pilots or ground troops at risk of injury, capture, or death. States with armed drones can conduct strikes without risking the lives of their own forces, which minimizes casualties, thereby reducing public outcry at home.

It is not surprising, in light of these advantages, that the use of armed drones has increased dramatically in conflict, and that the stated preference for capturing rather than killing suspected terrorists has been belied by a low capture-to-kill ratio. As part of a 2012 Department of Justice memo, the Obama administration highlighted what it deemed to be a restrictive set of conditions under which it would engage in targeted killings. In this memo, the administration stated that it would kill an individual who presented an "imminent threat" and if capture were not "feasible."[32] To be sure, it has seized some suspected militants. For example, the United States has detained a number of high-profile suspects through raids. In 2011, the United States seized Ahmed Abdulkadir Warsame, an interlocutor between Al-Shabab and Al-Qaeda in the Arabian Peninsula off Somalia, bringing him aboard the USS *Boxer*, where he was interrogated and then brought to New York for a trial. In 2013, the United States conducted a set of raids in Libya that captured Abu Anas Al-Liby, who had been accused of carrying out the 1998 East Africa embassy bombings and was later held in a secure location outside Libya and eventually taken to New York. He later died in custody in early 2015 from complications related to liver surgery, having contracted hepatitis C prior to his capture.[33]

These raids are more the exception than the rule, however. As of June 2014 fewer than 2% of the 473 non-battlefield-targeted killings have been conducted by raids or armed aircraft, with the remaining 98% by armed drones.[34] That these raids, arrests, and interrogations should be used when possible but have largely been avoided may seem surprising since raids help produce intelligence and are less controversial than killings. One reason for the preference for killing suspected terrorists over taking them captive is that it is not always clear what should be done with captured militants. Guantanamo Bay has been long been off the table in terms of accepting new detainees, and the process of trying suspected terrorists in US civilian courts remains fraught from a domestic politics standpoint, with members of Congress from the President's own party resisting trials in their own state or district. While some of the domestic political opposition is simply political theater, there are unresolved questions about the logistics of transporting suspected terrorists in terms of both security and safety. Against this backdrop of having few palatable options for dealing with suspected terrorists, killing rather than capturing has become the centerpiece of the United States' counterterrorism strategy.

Perhaps more importantly, arresting militants in the war zones and unstable areas where they are found is far riskier than killing via an unmanned drone. A pair of attacks in Somalia in October 2013 illustrates the difference. In early October, the same weekend as a Delta Force raid captured Al-Liby, SEAL Team Six landed in Somalia with the intention of capturing Abdulkadir Mohamed Abdulkadir (known as Ikrima), an Al-Shabab leader. The assault landed in failure, with the Special Forces encountering stiff resistance as well as women and children, leading them to withdraw after a firefight. Later that month, the United States returned to target Al-Shabab leaders with drones, killing Ibrahim Ali Abdi, a senior commander, and his friend in the attack. Thus, whereas capturing the targets may have been ideal, it was a higher risk proposition to the United States than the use of the unmanned drone that later went in and killed the suspected militant. Conversely, the low-risk proposition of an unmanned raid killed the suspected terrorist in the later (unmanned) case.

Q. Is the United States likely to continue using armed drones in combat?

As the above discussion suggests, drones present leaders and militaries with a number of advantages, most important of which are a long loiter time and minimized risk to troops. In this context, it is not surprising that the United States had established an impressive record for using drones and in some respects it is more surprising that its use of drone strikes had declined since the 2010 peak. Whether because it was exercising a more restrictive set of targeting rules or had run out of high-value targets, the United States had nonetheless throttled back its drone policy. The decline also seemed compatible with the attrition of a number of drone pilots, with the Air Force losing more drone pilots than it was training, thereby limiting the degree to which the United States could rely on drones.

In the middle of 2015, however, the Pentagon announced that it would increase the number of drone missions it conducted on a daily basis by 50%, from 60 to 90. These missions appeared to be primarily intended for surveillance and intelligence missions to monitor security in places such as Ukraine, Iraq, Syria, Northern Africa, and the South China Sea. With increasing tensions in these areas and with limits to the credibility of using military force against countries such as China and Russia, drones can offer a means of gathering intelligence while also showing a degree of force well below the threshold that would cause any retaliatory action. On the other hand, the mere presence of these American aircraft close to the drones' countries of interest could seem like a counterproductive provocation. Beyond the intelligence function that these missions would carry out, the vision implicit in plan was to increase the capacity to conduct lethal strikes, a more controversial proposition.

How the Pentagon will implement these increases when it had recently announced growing rates of attrition in its operator ranks remains to be seen. One way is to move from the near-exclusive reliance on the Air Force and toward greater reliance on the Army, which would contribute 16 flights per day, and Special Operations Command, which would contribute another four. The military also plans to rely more on enlisted personnel or private contractors at least to conduct surveillance or reconnaissance. The Pentagon would increase operational tempo gradually and in response to what it sees as a growing demand for drones in the world's hotspots.[35]

Q. Do drone strikes "work"?

If drone strikes do not work, then it makes little sense to consider the politics, legality, and ethics of their use. In other words, the deck would be so stacked against repeated strikes that drones would cease to be useful in a military capacity. The prevalent use of drones by the United States suggests that at least some high-level individuals think they have value. The Obama administration has repeatedly defended its use of drone strikes as "narrowly targeting our action against those who want to kill us," and even critics acknowledge that the use of armed drones has been successful in eliminating members of Al-Qaeda.[36] Perhaps the more vexing question though is not the tactical question of whether drone strikes have killed a number of suspected terrorists, a point on which most sides can agree, but the strategic question of whether this is an effective longer-term strategy. In other words, are drone strikes creating more terrorists than they kill?

The reasoning behind the possibility that drone strikes create more terrorists than they kill is as follows: Drone strikes taking place in areas such as Pakistan are seen by some individuals in those countries as a violation of sovereignty. The strikes also occasionally kill civilians, and the drones themselves are terrifying—imagine hearing the constant buzz of a drone overhead. As one individual indicated to *New Yorker* writer Steve Coll, "drones may kill relatively few but they terrify many more. They turned the people into psychiatric patients. The F-16s might be less accurate but they come and go."[37] According to this account, drones have alienated large numbers of the populace, causing individuals to take up arms against the perpetrators, in this case the United States. Drones then, based on this argument, create a backlash effect, killing some militants in the short term but creating far more in the long term.

There is much anecdotal evidence to this effect. In a 2012 tweet, a Yemeni lawyer wrote: "Dear Obama, when a US drone missile kills a child in Yemen, the father will go to war with you, guaranteed. Nothing to do with Al Qaeda." This view suggests that the motivation of revenge drives individuals to become militant, and not the ideology surrounding extremist Muslim groups. Another piece of evidence in this vein is the uptick of Al-Qaeda in the Arabian Peninsula (AQAP) members, which spiked in the years after drone strikes. AQAP consisted of a few hundred members in 2009, with no regional influence. By 2012 it had thousands of members and had control of some territory in Yemen.[38] Greg Johnsen, who has spent a considerable amount of time in Yemen, has concluded that drone strikes have helped recruitment of AQAP—they are the reason why the United States "lost Yemen." With a large number of strikes and a local base for training militants, Yemen has become a breeding ground for future terrorists.[39] The 2014 Nobel Peace Prize co-recipient for 2014, Malala Yousafzai, met with President Obama at the White House and expressed skepticism about the effectiveness of drone strikes, arguing that a more effective long-term strategy is to send books, not drones.

While this line of thinking is certainly compelling, critics counter that some threats are so imminent and potentially destructive that not eliminating them is more catastrophic than conducting a strike that might trigger a backlash over the longer term.[40] Others suggest that locals actually see these strikes as more benign than alternatives, such as the ground forces (whether the target country's or the United States'), which would likely displace large parts of the local population and destroy infrastructure.[41] This also seems to be a sustainable position. In fact, the two accounts could be fully compatible with each other if it means that in the short term, militants are killed but in the longer term, more militants are created. Leaders in a democracy might still have incentives to stop tomorrow's attack and then deal with the possibility of future attacks as they arise.

Investigating these two perspectives systematically is important since it bears on the types of counterterrorism and counter-radicalization efforts that would be needed alongside the drone strikes, and on the overall wisdom of the current policy. However, the question is a difficult one to evaluate empirically, the reason being that the location of strikes is not randomly distributed. They occur where there are militants, so looking at militant activity after a strike would not be independent of the reason why there were strikes in the first place. Saying that there is more militant activity in Waziristan after a strike compared to in Switzerland after no strike is not meaningful since the reason for the initial strike is that Waziristan was a breeding ground for terrorism.

Data on drone strikes presents challenges for this sort of comparison. Some scholars suggest that they can match an area with a strike against one without a strike and attribute differences in militant activity to the cause of the drone strike; these studies have found that drone strikes lower the incidence and lethality of terrorist attacks, though the studies cannot vouch for the long-term consequences, which would be important given that a blowback effect would be a longer-term proposition of recruitment, training, and planning a terrorist attack.[42] The finding directly challenges other studies that have shown a lower probability of organizational collapse than groups who have not lost their leaders.[43]

Although the empirical question of whether drone strikes create more terrorists than they kill is a difficult one to answer, there is certainly a plausible theoretical linkage between drone strikes and blowback, as well as persuasive qualitative evidence to this effect.[44] Given this possibility that the use of drone strikes contributes to radicalization, President Obama argued that "the use of force must be seen as part of a larger discussion we need to have about a comprehensive counterterrorism strategy," including the role of foreign assistance. Despite acknowledging the importance of this investment, budget requests for foreign assistance have seen little improvement in recent years, despite this being an area that could strengthen the populations that are turning to terrorism. At the least then, for those who see drone strikes as a tactical success, the potential adverse strategic consequences would warrant an offset through other means, including foreign assistance.

Q. Have American citizens been killed by drone strikes?

To date, the United States has killed about seven of its own citizens through drone strikes, three in Yemen and four in Pakistan. The strikes in Yemen were headlined by the killing of Anwar Al-Awlaki on September 11, 2011, making him the first US citizen to be killed in a US drone strike. According to US officials, Al-Awlaki was involved with Al-Qaeda as a recruiter and promoter of radical thought. He maintained a blog, a YouTube channel, and a magazine (*Inspire*), all of which are often cited as inspiration for terrorist attacks. At the time, he was central in organizing Al-Qaeda's foreign operations.[45] Attorney General Eric Holder wrote that, of the four US citizens killed in Yemen, only Al-Awlaki was intentionally targeted.[46]

While the others killed in Yemen were not deliberate targets, most had some suspected ties to terrorism. Al-Awlaki's son, Abdulrahman, who was born in Denver, Colorado, was killed on October 11, 2011. By all accounts, the strike was not targeting Abdulrahman; many US officials, including Barack Obama, were allegedly "surprised and upset" that Abdulrahman was killed.[47] Al-Awkali's son had no known ties to terrorism and was apparently out looking for his father, with the actual target supposedly being an Egyptian named Ibrahim Al-Banna, who was suspected of being a senior operative in Yemen's Al-Qaeda affiliate, AQAP.[48]

Samir Khan, on the other hand, who was killed in the same attack as Anwar Al-Awlaki, appeared to be somewhat more closely tied to terrorist activities. Khan, who was born in Riyadh, Saudi Arabia, had been raised in Queens, New York, later to move with his family to Charlotte, North Carolina. He had been maintaining a jihadist blog in his parents' basement when he moved to Yemen in 2009. There he became involved in the magazine, *Inspire*, the first online jihadi magazine in English writing in "a comfortable American vernacular," as the *New York Times* described it.[49] One passage declared that "it doesn't take a rocket scientist to figure out that I [am] Al Qaeda to the core."[50] Although not directly targeted in the strike that killed Aw-Awlaki, he would certainly have been on the radar of American counterterrorism officials.

There were two instances in which Americans were killed in Pakistani drone strikes. The first was on November 16, 2011, which killed Jude Kenan Mohammed. Mohammed was the son of an American mother and Pakistani father and grew up in North Carolina. In 2008, a few weeks before his 20th birthday, Mohammed left the United States to visit his father in Pakistan. He then disappeared in Pakistan, likely to join and train with Al-Qaeda. In 2009 Mohammed was placed on the FBI's Most Wanted list for providing material support to terrorists. The government reports that he was not specifically targeted, but clearly was considered to be of interest to the United States' counterterrorism officials.[51]

Although several of these individuals targeted seem like they were not merely in the wrong place at the wrong time, two others killed in Pakistan were just that. In April 2015, the United States reported that it had accidentally killed an American and an Italian, both aid workers who were being held hostage. The United States reported that it "had no reason to believe either hostage was present" during the operation, which intended to target two suspected American Al-Qaeda leaders who were thought to be in the compound. Despite near-continuous surveillance, the United States had not seen the hostages brought into the compound, thus inadvertently putting the two innocent individuals in the crosshairs.[52]

The same strike that killed the aid workers also killed Adam Gadahn, known as the American mouthpiece of Al-Qaeda for speaking against the country and in support of the terrorist organization. The US government reported that Gadahn was not a specific target but was in the Al-Qaeda compound that had been housing the aid workers who were also killed. A separate strike in April 2015 killed another American suspected of being an Al-Qaeda militant, named Ahmed Farouq, although he too was not specifically targeted.[53]

In his memoir, Panetta addressed at least the intentional killing of Americans, specifically that of Awlaki. He writes without remorse that Awlaki "actively and repeatedly took action to kill Americans and instill fear. He did not just exercise his rights of speech, but rather worked directly to plant bombs on planes and in cars, specifically intending those to detonate on or above American soil. He devoted his adult life to murdering his fellow citizens, and he was continuing that work at the time of his death."[54] In February 2013, a white paper seeking to clarify and institutionalize the general conditions for striking Americans was leaked to NBC News. That Department of Justice white paper sought to provide the legal reasoning behind targeting American citizens with drones.

The memo pointed to legal circumstances based on the belief that an individual is a "senior operational leader" of Al-Qaeda or "an associated force." Belief does not require specific intelligence about a plot to attack the United States. Indeed, the memo states that the United States does not need "clear evidence that a specific attack on US persons and interests will take place in the immediate future." The conceptualization was therefore thought to present "a more expansive definition of self-defense or imminent attack" than had been stated in public speeches.[55]

It was this question of targeting Americans that Senator Rand Paul used as the fulcrum for his filibuster of John Brennan's nomination as Director of the CIA. In one of the longest filibusters in recent Senate history, beginning at 11:47 am and ending around 12:30 am, Senator Paul raised the specter that drones were a threat to US citizens on US soil.[56] "No American should be killed by a drone on American soil without first being charged with a crime, without first being found guilty of a crime by a court," Paul said. "How can you kill someone without going to a judge, or a jury?"[57] When the filibuster ended, the vote to confirm Brennan proceeded and he became the next CIA director.

Less than a year later, news outlets reported that the US counterterrorism community was tracking an American working for Al-Qaeda and debating whether to target this individual. Although President Obama was due to make the final decision, on targeting Abdullah Al-Shami, translated as "Abdullah the Syrian," some members of Congress were allegedly informed. As Mazzetti and Schmitt put it, Abdullah Al-Shami's "nom de guerre masks a reality: He was born in the United States" before becoming a militant and fighting with Al-Qaeda in Pakistan.[58] The United States also moved aggressively to find Jehad Serwan Mostafa, another US citizen, thought to be involved with Al-Shabab in Somalia. The Justice Department offered a $5 million reward for information leading to his capture or conviction. Based on US policy, the killing would be justified if the alternative of capture was not feasible or if he was considered an imminent threat.

Q. Are drones just an unmanned version of other platforms or delivery systems?

One line of argument suggests that the killing of militants should not be attributed to the drone platform but rather the policy of targeted killings of suspected terrorists. Indeed, prominent scholars such as Charli Carpenter maintain that the real problem in terms of violations of international law is the policy of targeted killings and that drones, in and of themselves, are merely the delivery system that could just as easily be a soldier or a manned F-16.[59]

A number of military leaders have similarly suggested that drones are just another platform. In 2012, General Norton Schwartz, the chief of staff of the Air Force, stated that "if it is a legitimate target, then I would argue that the manner in which you engage that target, whether it be close combat or remotely, is not a terribly relevant question." Canada's chief of staff, General Thomas Lawson, made a similar comment in 2013: "If a kinetic round is propelled toward a confirmed enemy for strategic purposes by a rifle, by an artillery piece, by an aircraft manned, or an aircraft unmanned, any of those that end up with a desired effect is a supportable point of view."[60] Former Secretary of Defense Leon Panetta makes a similar argument in his memoirs: "to call our campaign against Al-Qaeda a 'drone program' is a little like calling World War I a 'machine gun program.' Technology has always been an aspect of war . . . what is most crucial is not the size of the missile or the ability to deploy it from thousands of miles away" but how the munitions are used.[61]

In assuming that lethal force is lethal force, what all of these assertions sidestep is the question of whether armed drones change the calculus surrounding the use of force. In other words, if a type of technology lowers the cost or risk of using force, then lethal force might still be lethal force, but there might be more of it. As a number of government leaders have acknowledged, drones have lowered the threshold for using force, and civilian and military leaders have been more willing to use force at times that they otherwise would have exercised more caution. As former Secretary of Defense Robert Gates noted, drones cause leaders to view war as "bloodless, painless, and odorless," allowing them to take liberties that would not be permissible were American casualties part of the calculation. As quoted in the *Washington Post*, he had come to see new technologies such as drones as providing an antiseptic form of warfare:

> Remarkable advances in precision munitions, sensors, information and satellite technology and more can make us overly enamored with the ability of technology to transform the traditional laws and limits of war. . . . A button is pushed in Nevada and seconds later a pickup truck explodes in Kandahar . . . [war is seen as] kind of video game or action movie. . . . In reality, war is inevitably tragic, inefficient and uncertain.[62]

The low risk to the operator and detachment from consequences on the battlefield make drones different. It makes them more tempting to employ than alternatives such as manned platforms or infantry, which involve more risk and bring individuals closer into contact with the tragic consequences of war. It is why targeted killings are conducted disproportionately by unarmed drones rather than manned aircraft or special forces and why the United States has killed rather than captured individuals even though capturing individuals can produce useful intelligence. The reason has to do with the fact that these vehicles are lower risk and will not incur casualties on the part of the state that uses them, and that they have high operational appeal in terms of their range, precision, and responsiveness. It is difficult then to disentangle altogether the technology and the policy, since the technology has advantages that allow it to be used in ways that lower the risk and in turn the threshold for using force.

Q. Are drones necessarily a game changer on the battlefield?

The inherent advantages of drones will not alone make traditional international warfare more likely—such conflicts are relatively rare anyway. Nor will the probable type, quantity, range, and lethality of armed drones that states possess in the coming decades make a government more likely to attempt to defeat an opposing army, capture or control foreign territory, or remove a foreign leader from power. Indeed, in 2015, after a year of using a combination of drones and manned airpower against ISIS in the Middle East, the United States and its allies were finding themselves unable to hold territory, which is a criticism of airpower more generally compared to ground forces.

In addition, a number of potential limitations stand in the way of drones becoming a ubiquitous game changer. They generally fly relatively slowly (the cruise speed of an F-16 is about three times that of a Reaper), and have therefore been described even by one Air Force general as "useless in a contested environment."[63] Countries with anti–air defense systems are well-positioned to shoot down the slow-moving drones. Hamas discovered this in 2014 when it flew what it referred to as an armed drone—very rudimentary—into Israel only to have the drone shot down. The current vulnerability to air defenses may also explain why Israel has not come to rely exclusively on armed drones in its conflicts. While drones are becoming more advanced, which means faster, stealthier, and able to fire more missiles, countries such as the United States and China are also developing technology that specifically targets drones, hoping to defang this emergent form of warfare.

Another source of vulnerability is that smaller drones must be linked by radio to their controller and the datalinks can be easily jammed and disabled. In an episode of the show 24, a United States drone is hacked and taken over by a terrorist that then tries to use the drone to kill the United States president. The plotline is not entirely science fiction. In one study, scholars showed how hackers could mimic GPS signals and fool the navigation systems. Drone cyberattacks could cause a drone, at the least, to be unable to calculate its position, causing it to be brought down fairly easily.[64] Responding to these vulnerabilities, the Defense Department has come up with a software program that is meant to ensure that the drone's control and navigation systems cannot be hacked. "Unhackable" seems a bit ambitious but is certainly the direction that drone software needs to go to address current vulnerabilities.

While drones are also developing better self-protection hardware systems or sensor capabilities to bring them in line with existing technologies, they are doing so only at a cost that many countries will not be able to afford. A stealth drone, for example, may be more useful and more resistant to this emerging technology, but will also be prohibitively expensive for all but a few countries. The Northrop Grumman–made Global Hawk, for example, lacked the U-2's system of defending against Russian-made air defense systems such as the S-300.[65] Upgrades that would bring the Global Hawk's defense system in line with U-2s was estimated to cost $1.9 billion over 10 years.[66] (That said, one government representative asserted that transitioning to the Global Hawk would bring longer-term savings because the U-2 costs $32,000 per flight hour compared to the Global Hawk at $24,000.[67])

Another reason why drones might not be transformative is that many of the capabilities of drones are also found in other systems. Helicopters, ballistic missiles, and manned aircraft can perform many of the same functions and are less vulnerable to anti-air defense systems. For terrorist groups, IEDs are likely simpler and more effective, and for groups such as

Hamas, a barrage of rockets would be better able to penetrate anti-air systems than a slow low-flying drone. As Davis and others indicate in their overview of drones for the Rand Corporation, "conventional technologies such as nil bombs and explosives are easier, cheaper, and can even be more lethal than drones." Take, for example, the 1995 Tokyo subway attack that killed 13 or the explosives on the London underground that killed 52.[68] Individuals seeking to wreak havoc or simply have a lethal impact could do more rapid harm with an assault rifle than a drone.

In some cases, manned alternatives bring superior capabilities. While the Reaper is an improvement over the Predator, for example, it is still less capacious than the A-10 or the F-16, which can carry bombs with more destructive power. In terms of raw weight, the Reaper's payload is about equivalent to that of the Army's Apache attack helicopter and a fraction of those of the A-10 (16,000 lb. or 7200 kg) and the F-16 (17,200 lb. or 7800 kg). However, it would be erroneous to equate payload weight to combat efficacy: the capabilities these payloads represent are quite different. As of now, the Reaper's principal armaments are the Hellfire air-to-ground missile and the Paveway II laser-guided bomb. While the drone is theoretically capable of carrying a Stinger air-to-air missile, factors such as limited range of view, aerodynamic limitations, and a lack of electronic countermeasures make the prospect of currently operational drones engaging in air-to-air combat an impossibility. The F-16, on the other hand, can effectively conduct both air-to-air and air-to-ground missions, a capability made possible in part by the range of the different classes of weapons the aircraft is designed to carry. Even the Apache and the A-10, both of which were principally designed to counter Soviet armored movements in Western Europe, can and have successfully engaged aerial targets. Furthermore, the three-manned aircraft discussed above are all equipped with a machine gun. While this may seem like a minor difference, cannons are highly versatile weapons systems, providing the ability to

conduct a variety of anti-personnel and anti-materiel operations. In short, the Predator, with its Hellfire II missiles (a
variant specifically designed to destroy above-ground structures), is uniquely suited for its current role of targeted killings and surveillance. In the event of a shooting war with a
conventional army, the limited survivability and versatility of
the current generation of unmanned systems limits some of
their tactical value.

Q. Is the use of armed drones legal under international law?

There is no legal prohibition against the use of armed drones.
Although there are movements to ban weaponized drones
through an anti-drone treaty, which will be discussed in subsequent sections, international institutions have generally
regarded drones in the spirit of saying that "drones don't kill
people, people kill people." In other words, international law
has essentially considered drones as another platform. Just as
an F-16 is legal as long as it is used in accordance with international law, so too is a drone.

The international legal questions that arise with drones are
not as much with the technology itself but rather how the drones
are used. And the questions about how armed drones are used
has been raised most saliently in the context of the United States,
which is reasonable given that it has been the country to use
armed drones most frequently. Insofar as state practice sets precedents in terms of how other states in the future use drones,[69]
examining these cases of armed drone strikes in terms of international legal compliance is quite reasonable. Indeed, CIA
Director John Brennan has remarked on how these principles
could lay the foundation for how other nations use drones. He
said that the administration's use of drones is "establishing precedents that other nations may follow, and not all of them will be
nations that share our interests. . . . If we want other nations to
use these technologies responsibly, we must use them responsibly. We cannot expect of others what we will not do ourselves."[70]

Critics have raised a number of legal and ethical questions about the United States' use of armed drones in combat. One set of questions deals with whether drone strikes comply with the recourse to force under international law (*jus ad bellum*, which means "right to war"). Indeed, the *jus ad bellum* concerns are about "the parameters of the war in which they're being used"—that is whether the United States is authorized to engage in armed attacks at all—rather than the technology itself.[71] Once a state has resorted to force, the vehicle through which states use force is less relevant than whether that force is proportional and distinguishes between civilian and combatant, an issue addressed later.

Under the UN Charter, there are two main circumstances under which states can use force: under Article 51, which is the right to collective or individual self-defense, and with a UN Security Council authorization. Otherwise, Article 2 (4) of the UN Charter proscribes intervention in other states' territories.

One view of drone strikes suggests that they are legal in active battlefields such as Afghanistan, Iraq, and Libya but also in places such as Pakistan, Yemen, and Somalia. This view has suggested that the United States is in fact engaged in a non-international armed conflict (NIAC) with the Taliban, Al-Qaeda, and its associates, and can target these forces where they exist. The supportive view also points to drone strikes as consistent with the principle of anticipatory self-defense, which customary international law interprets as a threat that is "instant, overwhelming, and leaving no choice of means, and no moment of deliberation." In its white paper on targeting suspected terrorists, the United States points to the importance of targeting imminent threats that are outside " 'hot' battlefields."[72]

A more restrictive view of this self-defense claim would say that the use of drones for targeting suspected terrorists outside "hot" battlefields such as Afghanistan violates the *jus ad bellum* principle of international law. Legal scholars such as Mary Ellen O'Connell dispute that the United States is engaged in an armed conflict with Pakistan, Yemen, and Somalia insofar as the hostilities are sporadic rather than a case of ongoing conflict, which would rule out the legality of drone strikes in these countries even if those countries consent.[73] More problematically, questions arise about whether the targets are compatible with anticipatory self-defense. Many of the targets have been lower-level foot soldiers—just 2% are "high-level targets"—who are "neither presently aggressing nor temporally about to aggress."[74]

Another line of critique about the use of drones in combat focuses on *jus in bello*, generally with respect to treatment of civilians and in particular whether combat drones are compatible with the principles of distinction and proportionality. The origins of both principles come from the just war tradition, which provided a set of philosophical and ethical guidelines for how actors would conduct themselves in conflict. These guidelines were later codified into the protocols that form the basis of international humanitarian law, which expects actors to discriminate between civilians and combatants, targeting the latter for military advantage and minimizing the damage to the former.[75]

According to the principle of distinction, actors are prohibited from directing their attacks against civilians. According to Article 48 of the Protocol Additional to the Geneva Convention (AP I), "In order to ensure respect for and protection of the civilian population and civilian objects, the Parties to the conflict shall at all times distinguish between the civilian population and combatants and between civilian objects and military objectives and accordingly shall direct their operations only against military objectives."[76] Beyond this provision, Article 57 of AP I requires that states "take all feasible precautions in the choice of means and methods of attack with a view to avoiding or in any event minimizing incidental loss of civilian life, injury to civilians and damage to civilian objects."[77]

Building on the principle of distinction, the principle of proportionality suggests that the anticipated military gain of a strike must exceed the anticipated damage to civilians and their property. Article 51 (5) (b) of AP I proscribes "an attack which may be expected to cause incidental loss of civilian life, injury to civilians, damage to civilian objects, or a combination thereof, which would be excessive in relation to the concrete and direct military advantage anticipated."[78] As the former Prosecutor of the International Criminal Court, Luis Moreno-Ocampo, suggested, "the death of civilians does not in itself constitute a war crime." It must be intentional and must exceed the anticipated military advantage.

Members of the policy and legal community have debated at length whether drone strikes meet the principles of distinction and proportionality under *jus in bello*. As Max Boot states, "[t]he US military operates a bewildering array of sensors to cut through the fog of war."[79] Military documents themselves point to the way that technology facilitates the kind of awareness that would help comply with international legal principles. The military's Joint Vision 2010 notes that "in all operations technological advances ... allow them [the warfighters] to make better decisions."[80] The precision capabilities of an armed Predator or Reaper that can loiter over targets and carry precision munitions are an improvement over earlier alternatives such as carpet-bombing. Drones may also be an improvement over alternatives, such as the use of ground forces or air strikes. In his collection of data from drone strikes, Avery Plaw suggests that civilian fatalities from the use of drones are comparatively lower than either non-drone US operations or Pakistani ground operations in FATA, suggesting that drone strikes are more proportional than the alternatives, or at least less disproportional. He concludes that "a fair-minded evaluation of the best data we have available suggests that the drone program compares favorably with similar operations and contemporary armed conflict more generally."[81]

Other accounts of US targeting are less charitable in terms of its compliance with the laws of war. Technology, in the form of better sensors, may produce intelligence that can help inform high-stakes decisions, which otherwise could be too risky without sufficient surveillance information. Additionally, the development in the precision of weapons has proved more effective in both hitting the designated target and causing less incidental damage. However, it cannot make the subtle distinctions necessary for adjudicating the fine line between a civilian and a combatant. This exposes the problem with assertions made by individuals such as CIA Director John Brennan that "one of the things President Obama has insisted on is that we're exceptionally precise and surgical in terms of addressing the terrorist threat." The implication is that precision means distinction and proportionality in hitting the terrorists and sparing damage to others, erroneously implying that technology can be the last word on judgments about context and identity.

Inherent in these judgments is the often-subjective question of who is a combatant and therefore a legal target and who is a civilian and therefore not a legal or legitimate target. As earlier sections suggest, drone strikes have indeed killed a number of civilians, but the percentages vary widely. One of the reasons why these accounts and percentages vary widely is because of fluid interpretations of who is defined as an illegal civilian target and who is defined as a legal combatant target, creating challenges in terms of ascertaining exactly who is a combatant and who is a civilian. Part of the problem resides in the ambiguity of Article 4 of the Geneva Conventions, which designates an individual as a combatant in part by "having a fixed distinctive emblem recognizable at a distance." The 1977 AP I states that "civilians shall enjoy the protection afforded by this section, unless and for such time as they take a direct part in hostilities."[82]

Conventional wars such as World War II made these criteria quite clear, since combatants were generally wearing uniforms. Modern unconventional conflict creates situations where combatants are not clearly identifiable based on emblems, and are often oscillating between direct and indirect participant and civilian. The commingling makes it difficult to discern legitimate combatants from protected civilians.[83] Applying the standard to counterterrorist situations is therefore quite fraught with difficulties. The International Committee of the Red Cross has sought to offer clear guidance on the difference between direct and indirect participation, but even their legal experts have had challenges coming to a consensus. As the Israeli High Court of Justice's Judgment on Targeted Killings reported, "the notion of direct participation in hostilities is complex, emotive, and still inadequately resolved."[84] Its own view is that the "direct" character of the part taken should not be narrowed merely to the person committing the physical act of attack but should also include people in the business of intelligence and transportation of those who do carry out those attacks. By this measure, almost anyone in a community could wittingly or unwittingly be in a position to be considered as having a direct involvement in hostilities.[85]

That the definition can be quite subjective explains in part the wide variation among accounts of civilian casualties, as discussed earlier. For example, many cases of individuals killed are ambiguous, with press reports referring to "people killed" or "unknown" status, making it difficult to difficult to know whether to put those individuals in the numerator (civilian) or denominator (total). Indeed, this is one reason the government can claim zero civilian casualties but have that position be disputed by studies involving interviews of individuals on the ground near the attacks, where people might have a different understanding of the role the target had played in hostilities.

As this section suggests, the international legal questions surrounding the use of drones have hinged on both questions of sovereignty (*jus ad bellum*) and concerns about damage to civilians (*jus in bello*). With concerns in mind that its drone attacks had not been compatible with international law, the United States has, in recent years, gone to greater lengths to clarify its policies on the use of armed drones. In a talk at Northwestern School of Law, then–Attorney General Eric Holder outlined the legal basis for using lethal force in counterterrorism operations abroad, saying that the operations would be consistent with law of war principles.[86] Holder spoke to the questions of sovereignty, arguing that "because the United States is in an armed conflict, we are authorized to take action against enemy belligerents under international law ... and international law recognizes the inherent right of national self-defense. None of this is changed by the fact that we are not in a conventional war." He thus outlined arguments both about being in a NIAC and also relating to self-defense in terms of striking individuals outside places such as Afghanistan.

In a major speech a year later, President Obama continued the legal defense, arguing that strikes are conducted only against targets considered to be "a continuing and imminent threat to the American people," in areas "where there are no other governments capable of effectively addressing the threat" and where there is "near-certainty that no civilians will be killed or injured."[87] This major speech gave the sense that the terms of counterterrorism operations had narrowed, and it does appear that there are fewer strikes than there had been during their peak in 2010. That the United States has felt compelled to respond to these legal concerns is indicative of the quite-vociferous opposition that the strikes had elicited. Nongovernmental organizations such as Amnesty International and international organizations such as the United Nations remain concerned that the United States targets individuals in ways that it deems extrajudicial or at least pushing the boundaries of international law.

Q. Is the use of armed drones ethical?

The use of armed drones presents a complex moral calculus. One view suggests that if a state uses force as part of its counterterrorism policy, then the most humane, ethical way to carry it out is through the use of drone strikes. As Dan Byman points out, drone strikes are more ethical than many tools host nations would use to deal with terrorist organizations. The Yemeni and Pakistani militaries, for example, have a history of torturing detainees and indiscriminately bombing civilian areas.

Bradley Strawser has also defended the use of drones on ethical and moral grounds, suggesting that drones are more accurate in terms of reducing casualties on the ground and do not bring a pilot into the line of fire. As he and others have suggested, drones are not novel in terms of their ability to engage targets lethally and if anything are a more appropriate vehicle than predecessors or existing alternatives. Strawser suggests that if a country is going to engage in conflict, drones are the most humane, legal way to do it. Indeed, "using such technology is, in fact, obligatory."[88]

On the other side of the debate are philosophers who have raised the question about whether drones introduce a moral hazard for the use of force.[89] Moral hazards involve situations whereby avoiding cost has the perverse incentive of causing one actor to engage in risks that they would not otherwise take. Consider, for instance, that in 2014, 70% of skiers report wearing helmets—triple the number from 2003. Still the number of head injuries has not declined. The hunch is that helmets give individuals license to take more risks, exposing them to injuries that even helmets cannot protect against.[90]

The metaphor about costs and risks applies in the context of drones; drones present no costs to the user. The drone operators are not at risk and the domestic populace does not see body bags coming home from war. The result, backed by comments of many former leaders, including former Secretaries of Defense Gates and Panetta, is that the use of drones has allowed the United States to take liberties with using force precisely because the technology is relatively antiseptic and low-cost.[91] According to this formulation, the problem is not so much with how a particular side uses force, but *that* it is using force. The counterfactual question it raises is whether that actor would have engaged in force in the absence of the enabling technology. That the United States has engaged in armed drone strikes with the frequency it has, and to the near-exclusion of manned alternatives, suggests a counterfactual world with lower levels of military force. It is this moral hazard problem—an unintended consequence of a low-cost technology being that it is used less discerningly—that presents the alternative ethical perspective.

It is on this side of the philosophical debate that theorists such as Michael Walzer wade in. Walzer worries that to those equipped with a hammer, everything will look like a nail, and in the case of having armed drones, everything will look like a viable, legitimate target. He notes that "here is the difficulty: the technology is so good that the criteria for using it are likely to be steadily relaxed," causing an "overuse of drones" and tendency to use drones as a blunt instrument rather than as a vehicle for precise, targeted killing. He concludes that using drones in this way isn't "morally wise," and implies that bearing some risk ourselves could help create a more circumspect and moral targeting strategy.[92] Such guidance, of course, runs counter to one key reason why leaders have found drones to be attractive, which is that they minimize risk to one's own side, but from the purely ethical standpoint of just war theory, militaries must be willing to sacrifice not just for their own troops but for civilians in areas where they are engaged in conflict.

Q. Is there major opposition to the use of armed drones?

As the use of armed drones grew in frequency between 2005 and 2010, a number of groups began forming an anti-drone coalition in protest. What unifies this movement is a commitment to nonviolence in the service of, at the most extreme, banning all drones through an international treaty, and, more modestly, reducing reliance on drones and creating more accountability. The movement has gained international attention, with 75,000 individuals having signed a petition that would take a number of actions against the use of drones, including an international ban on the use or sale of weaponized drones, but also international action under the International Criminal Court to investigate those who have carried out drone attacks.

The international movement has had national-level followings as well. In the United States, the most visible group in the movement is Global Drones Watch run by Code Pink Women for Peace, which describes itself as a grassroots organization working to end US-funded wars. The group organized a 2013 summit in Washington, DC with delegates from Yemen, Afghanistan, and Germany and sought to highlight the casualties that have resulted from American drone strikes. Other groups in the United States have also joined the anti-drone movement. For example, a group called Iraq Veterans Against the War placed an anti-drone advertisement in the *Air Force Times* in 2015 urging drone pilots, sensor operators, and support teams to become conscientious objectors in the United States' armed drone strikes, arguing that these armed drone strikes and surveillance missions violate international law.

Although the use of drones is generally popular among legislators, isolated members of Congress have voiced concerns about the use of drones, though generally in the context of the homeland. Senator Rand Paul's (R-KY) filibuster of President Obama's 2013 nomination of John Brennan for the Director of the CIA focused primarily on targeting Americans and primarily with force (though also through surveillance), and had little to say about the appropriateness of using armed drones abroad. Some members of Congress such as Congressman Adam Schiff (D-CA) have also questioned the CIA's dominant role in conducting the armed drone strikes in places such as Yemen and Pakistan, asking whether there is adequate oversight compared to the Joint Special Operations Command; nevertheless, the CIA has remained the government agency responsible for most strikes. In short, opposition to the executive's drone policy has largely been silent in the legislative branch.

The anti-drone movement has local roots, however, often at locations proximate to drone bases. For example, groups in upstate New York, many of which have connections with Catholic pacifist groups, near Hancock Airfield outside Syracuse have protested the use of this base to carry out attacks in Afghanistan. Several acts of civil disobedience have landed many of the protesters in local jails. One prominent example that made national headlines featured Mary Anne Grady Flores, a grandmother of four living in Ithaca, NY, who was sentenced to jail for a year for participating in a protest outside Hancock Airfield after being instructed by the local courts to desist.

Q. What is it like to be a drone pilot?

Initially, many drone operators were reassigned from piloting other aircraft whether because of physical obstacles in the way of flying airplanes, e.g., eyesight problems, age, or because of backlogs in training for the manned aircraft they were taught to fly. Individuals would then go to the Predator schoolhouse for Initial Qualification Training (IQT), just as other new pilots would go to IQT for F-15 Eagles, C-17 tankers, or B-1 bombers. No longer does the Air Force send individuals from undergraduate pilot training directly to drone training. The most significant problem with individuals going to pilot training and then to drones was financial. It costs the taxpayers about $1.5M to produce one traditional pilot. One fully qualified drone pilot can be trained for much less than that.

As of the beginning of 2013, Air Force pilots either transitioned from another weapons system or went through drone-specific training in a new specialty code for "Attack RPA Pilot." Training would include 25 hours of manned, powered flight, then training on the unmanned Predator or Reaper. Operating drones has some appeal for individuals. As one former drone pilot reported, "there is an honorable element. We do good work. We produce tactical effects for combatant commanders. We kill enemies and save friends." He went on to say that since drone operators are "perpetually at war," they can have more impact—seen as an upside of being a drone pilot—than the manned pilots who deploy for 4 months and then return for 8 to 12 months.[93]

Despite this appeal to some, mainstream military culture is still somewhat antithetical to the business of drone operations.

The same drone operator said, "those of us who wanted to fly traditionally manned aircraft wanted to be Maverick or Ice Man [from the movie Top Gun]. There is a man-machine interface, but there is still a 'cowboy' kind of mentality. It is the front line, the tip of the spear of the AF. Sitting on the ground in a trailer does not satisfy this desire." The shift work is onerous, doing the same thing day in and day out, which is not what many individuals envisioned when they joined the military. As a result, "drone operators are leaving the Air Force in droves,"[94] the tempo of operation being exhausting and overwhelming. Manning rates for drone pilots have been less than 50% compared to 84% for pilots in the Air Force overall, prompting the Air Force to explore new policies such as opening up Global Hawk operations to enlisted personnel.

A 2013 report by the Armed Forces Health Surveillance Center examined the health records of 709 drone pilots and 5,256 manned aircraft pilots between October 2003 and December 2011. Those conducting the study expected that drone operators would have higher incidence rates of mental health disorders such as post-traumatic stress disorder (PTSD), as drone operators "witness the carnage. Manned aircraft pilots don't do that. They get out of there as soon as possible."[95] Yet the report concluded that controlling for factors such as age, time in service, and number of deployments, the incidence rates for 12 mental health conditions including post-traumatic stress disorder were similar for drone pilots as manned platforms. Stress rates were higher for drone pilots than for those in logistics or support jobs, however. Forty-six percent of Reaper and Predator pilots and 48% of Global Hawk sensor operators report high stress at their jobs, citing long and inconsistent working hours as a potential cause. One Air Force Predator pilot corroborated these accounts: "the grind got to me. Same thing day in and day out (for the most part). The perpetual shift work was rough. And there was no sign that it was going to get any better."[96]

While the stress rates of drone pilots were relatively higher than those for other members of the Air Force, such as those in logistics and support roles, the rates of mental health problems for pilots of both manned and unmanned platforms were reportedly lower. The Armed Forces Health Surveillance Center report suggests that this may be the result of underreporting, with pilots (both manned and unmanned) concerned that mental health problems could disqualify them from flying. The Center plans to conduct two follow-up studies: one to try to work around the pilots' possible underreporting of mental health symptoms, and another that looks at the mental health of the support staff who work alongside the drone pilots controlling the cameras.[97] While these are fruitful next steps, other important areas of the study would include comparisons between operators who pilot drones for the military versus the CIA, and the operational stress levels experienced by unmanned versus manned pilots.

Monotony is clearly one of the factors contributing to operator dissatisfaction and stress—especially for the many individuals who joined the military with the expectation of being fighter jocks. There have even been several efforts to address the cultural distance between being a manned aircraft pilot and a drone operator. Some units have tried to bring some of the traditional flying culture into drone operations, though, by most accounts it is difficult to change the sense that the operators are playing the role of robots themselves, surveying the ground for long, monotonous shifts. Plans to introduce a Distinguished Warfare Medal for drone operators and cyberwarriors were scuttled after two months because of a sense among members of Congress and some veterans "that it was unfair to make the medal a higher honor than some issued for valor on the battlefield."[98] The medal was originally proposed by outgoing Defense Secretary Leon Panetta to honor those who were making a difference in combat from afar. Yet it was Chuck Hagel, who upon assuming his position as Defense Secretary on April 15, 2013, replaced the medal with a "new distinguishing device that can be affixed to existing medals to recognize the extraordinary actions of this small number of men and women."[99]

At least in terms of numbers, the potential pool of recipients is not actually small. The Air Force has trained more drone pilots since 2008 than fighter and bomber pilots combined; by 2015 this means there will be more individuals trained to fly drones than bombers.[100] Higher training rates, however, are essential given that drone pilots have left the service at three times the rate of pilots of manned aircraft, though some aviation analysts have suggested that a more appropriate approach is to follow that of the Army, which allows warrant officers with just a high school diploma to fly unmanned aircraft and helicopters. Drone pilots clearly occupy an uneasy space in a culture dominated by manned pilots, suggesting changes to the drone operator culture and training or changes to the service culture as a whole, either of which presents challenges. Trying to address the drone culture runs up against structural obstacles as there is an interest in maintaining the prestige as an officer-only specialty while dealing with the fact that the job entails unenviable shift work.

Given the Pentagon's plans to shift more drone operations to the Army, the question arises whether that service is better equipped to fly drone missions. Army drone pilots face somewhat different sets of constraints. One is that they are often pulled over to non-drone activities, including guard duty and even lawn care, which has made it difficult for the Army pilot to stay current with their training hours.[101] Part of the problem is that while the Air Force has a fighter pilot culture, the Army has a culture that is not organized primarily around flying, let alone unmanned platforms. The greater reliance on the Army then would require a different set of kinks to be ironed out, which says nothing about the quite secretive Special Operations Command, which has carried out drone strikes in places such as Somalia and Yemen and would be assuming a greater role in the vision for more daily surveillance and strike missions.

Q. How does the use of drones affect democratic checks and balances?

In the United States, the responsibility for authorizing military force resides with Congress, yet the relationship between the use of drones and Congressional checks in wartime is uneasy at best. This is in large part due to the rapid development of drone technology that shifts the burdens of war away from the populace. Immanuel Kant famously observed that what makes democracies different from non-democracies is that the polities of the former directly bear the burdens of war. Since they have to fight these wars and pay the costs, their consent for the war is heavily contingent on how they see the virtues of fighting the war, and then put pressure on the government as soon as they no longer see the war as worth the ongoing sacrifice.[102]

Contemporary international relations scholars have followed up in this vein and suggested that since a democratic populace will "ultimately pay the price of war in higher taxes and bloodshed," they will "sue for peace" when the costs mount, creating shorter wars at lower cost.[103] The accountability mechanism underlying this logic hinges on the public bearing some burden of war. With drone strikes, however, the public is removed from the consequences. Indeed, insofar as all politics is local and one's family and friends are not coming home in body bags, then the incentive to pressure leaders to end wars diminishes.[104]

It is not surprising that the domestic public in the United States, the country which operates the most drones, expresses greater levels of support for drone strikes after ten years than they do for the Afghanistan war after ten years.[105] Indeed, the American public has generally been supportive of drone strikes, with support rarely falling below 50% for polls taken between 2011 and 2014 (while the first strike was in 2002, polls did not begin until 2011) and typical support levels reaching around 65%.

By contrast, Americans are overwhelmingly concerned about drone use domestically, especially when it comes to their own privacy. Sixty-four percent of Americans have indicated that they would be very or somewhat concerned if law enforcement used drones for surveillance and 67% are opposed to drones being used for routine policing.[106] Americans also express skepticism about the use of drones for commercial purposes by a 2-1 margin in opposition, with only 21% in favor—the remaining 35% neither supportive nor opposed.

Most significantly, Congress has not specifically authorized the use of drone strikes outside active battle-fields. In 2001 it passed the Authorization for the Use of Military Force (AUMF), which authorized the President to "use all necessary and appropriate force against those nations, organizations, or persons he determines planned, authorized, committed, or aided the terrorist attacks that occurred on September 11, 2001, or harbored such organi-zations or persons, in order to prevent any future acts of international terrorism against the United States by such nations, organizations or persons." While both Presidents Bush and Obama have implicitly used the AUMF to legiti-mize drone strikes in places such as Pakistan, Yemen, and Somalia, a legal debate has evolved dealing with whether the 2001 AUMF intended to be open-ended in both time and space. Does Al-Shabab in Somalia, for example, qual-ify under the AUMF? The group was not present at the time of 9/11 but ostensibly had been placed within the Al-Qaeda network since its inception. Ryan Goodman pointed out as much after the September 2014 strike against the leader of Al-Shabab, Ahmed Abdi Godane, by questioning whether the group is an "associated force" of Al-Qaeda. The answer to this question provides or denies the United States the legal authority to target members of Al-Shabab. Despite the unclear ground upon which the United States is making attacks against Al-Shabab, there has been little Congressional opposition to strikes against them on these grounds.[107] While President Obama himself urged the repeal of the AUMF, stating that he "look[s] forward to engaging Congress and the American people in efforts to refine, and ultimately repeal, the AUMF's mandate" he has not identified a replacement that would authorize the type of strikes that have been allegedly carried out with this authorization.

In other cases, such as the Libya intervention, the Obama administration claimed that it did not have to seek authorization for military force because it was only using drones, thereby exempting it from the 1973 War Powers Resolution, which would require Congressional authorization in the event that troops were deployed for more than 60 days. It stated that "U.S. operations do not involve sustained fighting or active exchanges of fire with hostile forces, nor do they involve U.S. ground troops" and do not obligate the United States to seek specific authorization.[108]

In the 2014 strikes against ISIS in Iraq and Syria, the administration appeared to act on the basis of Article II of the US Constitution, which grants commander-in-chief privileges to the president. Former legal advisor to the president Harold Koh suggested that the government has relied on the "splinter theory" that allows it to use force based on the "associated forces" part of the AUMF. The basic argument suggests that the AUMF authorized the President to engage in an armed counterterrorism campaign, and that since the 9/11 attacks, the original Al-Qaeda group has splintered into other groups, some of which may have had different objectives, but bore enough resemblance to the parent group to be culpable and subject to being targeted under the original AUMF.[109]

Consistent with this logic, the executive branch has continued to engage in strikes against organizations that are new since 9/11, such as ISIS, AQAP, and Al-Qaeda in the Islamic Maghreb (AQIM), and that remain unchecked by the legislative branch.

On the contrary, Congress has been loath to restrict the president's autonomy when it comes to using armed drones for counterterrorism. Some individuals, such as Congressman Adam Schiff (D-CA), have proposed a sunset clause for the AUMF but these measures have gained little traction. Congress has little incentive to introduce meaningful restrictions. While it is unlikely to get credit for foreign policy successes, it would be blamed if it introduced restrictions and a terrorist attack took place. Its incentives then are to grant the executive branch considerable latitude when it comes to counterterrorism policy, especially since the status quo comes at no real cost to the constituents the members of Congress represent.

3

PROLIFERATION OF DRONES TO OTHER COUNTRIES

As earlier chapters suggest, the United States has been, by far, the country leading the use of armed drones. Having used drones first in Afghanistan in 2001, in Yemen in 2002, then in Pakistan in 2004, the United States has come to rely on drones as a technology that offers the ability to loiter over targets and strike without inflicting casualties, giving it both operational and domestic political advantages. Other countries have looked at the United States' experience and seen the advantages of using drones in combat, and many have adopted the technology or at least explored the possibility of developing it or acquiring it from other drone-producing countries. This section explores those proliferation dynamics and the possible consequences.

Q. Which other countries have drones?

The Government Accountability Office reports that between 2005 and December 2011 the number of countries with drones went from 41 to 76. While the number is a dramatic increase, the report goes on to say that most of these foreign drones are tactical limited-range drones that are not used in the service of armed force but rather in collecting intelligence and surveillance.[1] Indeed, a 2015 study by the Center for New American Security reported that 87 countries were operating drones, but that this number included countries such as Trinidad and Tobago that were flying tactical systems, a far cry from the type of drones the United States has used for counterterrorism strikes.[2]

According to a 2014 Rand Corporation report, eight countries are developing the so-called Category I drones that the MTCR believes are most sensitive and advanced: China, India, Iran, Russia, Taiwan, Turkey, the United Arab Emirates (UAE), and the United States. Three countries are developing the Category II systems that are seen as less sensitive systems: Israel, Pakistan, and South Africa. The Ababil developed by Iran has reportedly been exported to Hezbollah and possibly Venezuela.[3] Israel, which exported about $4.6 billion in drones between 2005 and 2012, exceeding US exports by $1.6 billion, remains a leader in the production and export of drones, with the majority of the world drone exports (41%) originating in Israel and ending up in as many as 24 countries. Israel also owns drone-manufacturing subsidiaries that are based in the United States. For example, Stark Aerospace, based in Mississippi, sells Hunter drones through Northrop Grumman but is a US subsidiary of Israel Aerospace Industries.[4] It mainly exports commercial drones but is an example of a country that has enough technical and financial strength to easily move into manufacturing Category I drones. Twelve other countries are developing systems that do not fall into Category I or II: France, Germany, Greece, Italy, Lebanon, North Korea, South Korea, Spain, Sweden, Switzerland, Tunisia, and the United Kingdom.

Other countries are interested in advanced drones but have not produced them and have therefore made the move to import the technology. In July 2013, Congress approved the export of up to 16 unarmed Reapers to France. France was fighting Ansar Dine, a group of jihadist insurgents, in Mali. Because Ansar Dine had no air defenses, France was able to successfully use Reapers for increased situational awareness and make advances against the rebel group. Reapers have a number of visual sensors, including an infrared sensor and two TV cameras, making it ideal for acquiring and relaying visual information. They are able to cruise at approximately 230 miles per hour and have a range of up to 1,150 miles from their control site. Spain, Italy, and the Netherlands also ordered the Reaper; the United Kingdom remains the only country to whom the United States has exported the armed Reaper, although the US State Department reported in November 2015 its plans to weaponize Italy's drones.[5] Several European countries remain interested in jointly developing a European drone but that remains under study.[6]

For US partners such as Iraq, drones are even more appealing. Iraq has no indigenous military production and must therefore import its technology, yet does not confront sophisticated air defense systems that might threaten slow-flying drones. The Scan Eagle and helicopter-like Fire Scout drones have therefore been useful for conducting surveillance for its ongoing security operations as well as to monitor the transfer of Iraqi oil from the oil fields that were inland to tankers in the Gulf. The State Department was careful to note that it was "not even feasible" that the drones could be armed. Reports suggest that China may have sold an armed drone to Iraq, however.[7]

Another category of countries aspiring to acquire military drones are those more interested in the surveillance and reconnaissance capabilities of drones such as the Global Hawk. Australia is keeping open "an option for a future force," while several Asian countries have pursued the Global Hawk, which Japan has argued it needs so that it may "counter China's growing assertiveness at sea, especially when it comes to the Senkaku Islands."[8]

In short, while the total number of countries with drones has increased dramatically in the last decade, the subset of countries that has the more advanced drones is far more limited. Nonetheless, that dynamic is beginning to change, as more countries produce or import drones with greater range, endurance, and payload that can cross borders and conduct strikes.

Q. Will there be a drones "arms race"?

A report by the Teal Group predicts an increase in worldwide spending on drone procurement and research and development (R&D) from $6.6 billion in 2013 to $11.4 billion in 2022.[9] Currently, US spending on R&D accounts for more than half of the worldwide spending on these ventures. The Teal Group report predicts that the United States' drone budget will increase only slightly by 2022 compared to the rise in other countries' expenditures.

Despite the increased interest in drones, the outcome may not be the arms race that some observers have predicted. In 2011, for example, the *New York Times* headline blared: "Coming Soon—The Drone Arms Race"; the piece opened with the line: "what was a science-fiction scenario not much more than a decade ago has become today's news."[10] Today's news though meant that US strikes in Iraq, Afghanistan, Pakistan, Yemen, and other countries have left other countries rushing to catch up. As one defense analyst observed, "virtually every country on earth will be able to build or acquire drones capable of firing missiles within the next ten years. Armed aerial drones will be used for targeted killings, terrorism and the government suppression of civil unrest. What's worse, say experts, is that it's too late for the United States to do anything about it."[11] Such prognostications ignore several natural obstacles that stand in the way of the ubiquitous proliferation of advanced armed drones.

First, while some observers have suggested that stopping "the spread of drone technology will prove impossible [because they] are highly capable weapons that are easy to produce," another perspective suggests the spread of the more lethal, capacious technology will not necessarily be so easily diffused.[12] These two perspectives could be compatible on some level. Indeed, anyone can go online and buy a rudimentary drone, so these could easily and quickly diffuse, and smaller-scale tactical drones have proliferated quickly as the previous sections suggest. These drones can create disruptions, but do not pose the same lethality as the type of drones that are of concern in terms of proliferation, such as the Predator or Reaper that are long-range and capable of high impact lethal strikes.

On the contrary, the technology required for advanced armed drones may be out of reach except to the most advanced militaries. Developing an advanced armed drone such as a Reaper requires complex engineering to fully develop the complex web of aircraft design, precise missile systems, operating systems, and stealth that makes for effective drones. Even fairly sophisticated militaries have struggled to produce the type of advanced armed drone that the United States has used in combat. Russia, for example, has had its efforts to acquire more advanced drones thwarted by technical challenges. In one case in January 2010, an armed drone prototype of the Stork drone crashed and burned as it attempted takeoff, effectively ending the program. Russia is thought to be about 20 or more years behind the United States, with the prospect of a combat drone that can replace its Cold War–era Tupolev bombers not scheduled to be ready for combat until at least 2040.[13]

Several European countries, such as France and Italy, which have expressed an interest in armed drones, have not been able to produce the technology through their development efforts. This has limited them to employing unarmed versions of the United States' Reaper. A consortium of Airbus, Dassault, and Alenia Aermacchi has been looking to develop a medium-altitude, long-endurance drone by 2020. The group has struggled to meet common requirements across countries, making the target date less and less feasible. The partnership between France and the United Kingdom to develop a Future Combat Air System is in the development stage but will not test demonstrators until the 2020s with a system fielded in the 2030s.[14]

A second obstacle standing in the way of an inexorable march toward a world of armed drones is that while the domestic populace in a country such as the United States favors armed drone strikes as a way to minimize risk to their own troops, the situation in other countries can look quite differ-ent. Leaders advocating the acquisition of armed drones have experienced intense opposition, with the public leery of violat-ing the defensive security posture that is ingrained in Europe's post–World War II identity. In Germany, for example, the pros-pect of armed drones has produced an animated debate about the ethics and strategic implications of using armed drones, with those on the left arguing that armed drones would lower "the political threshold for using force," causing Germany to use force in "increasingly remote regions of the earth," and therefore should not be part of Germany's arsenal.[15] Signaling similar reservations about the use of armed drones, in February 2014, the European Parliament passed a declaration seemingly oriented toward the United States but presumably applying to its own defense posture, saying that "drone strikes outside a declared war by a state on the territory of another state without the consent of the latter or of the UN Security Council constitute a violation of international law and of the territorial integrity and sovereignty of that country."[16] That European leaders are not enamored with drone strikes sug-gests that the permissive domestic politics environment of the United States may not be replicated elsewhere.

A third factor that might impede the diffusion of advanced armed drones is that they might not be seen as producing a high enough payoff when taking into account the costs and benefits. While their unit costs have come down in the United States, many countries would find the costs of investing in unmanned technology within their own defense sector to be prohibitive. Indeed, the European experience with the unmanned Euro Hawk, which was cancelled in 2013 because of high costs, may be instructive. Having spent about $750 million in the project, the countries involved cut their losses when it became clear that the unmanned aircraft did not have the required "sense and avoid systems" that avoid collisions in the European Union, or lightning and icing protection required by NATO. Not only does the prospect of new development systems come with high costs—some of which become known only over the course of development—the benefits are not entirely clear. To be sure, having an armed drone reduces the human costs of war to the state using the technology, but from a purely operational perspective, countries might be satisfied with having an armed equivalent (e.g., an F-16) or a cruise missile that does not incur the same investment costs.

A fourth reason why the diffusion of armed drones may not take the form of an arms race is that countries unable to produce armed drones indigenously cannot simply go to an international arms bazaar and purchase them. Indeed, while the international institutional mechanisms under the MTCR are not perfect, they do impact the availability of supply, decreasing access to armed drones. Thus, early prognostications about nuclear proliferation—which proved wildly pessimistic because nonproliferation initiatives ended up reducing the supply of materials needed to stockpile nuclear weapons—might serve as an appropriate guidepost for armed drone proliferation. In 1960 presidential candidate John F. Kennedy had predicted that there would be 20–25 nuclear countries by the end of the decade. In the third presidential debate he claimed: "there are indications because of new inventions, that 10, 15, or 20 nations will have a nuclear capacity, including Red China, by the end of the Presidential office in 1964. This is extremely serious... I think the fate not only of our own civilization, but I think the fate of world and the future of the human race, is involved in preventing a nuclear war."[17] Yet with the growing nonproliferation movement, pressures increased to limit the horizontal proliferation of nuclear weapons so that by the end of the decade there were only five countries in possession of nuclear weapons. In other words, nuclear technology was also thought to be diffusing quickly and yet efforts to stem proliferation through limiting the supply were successful. The historical analogy could prove apt in the case of advanced armed drones, whose availability may be curtailed by international institutions such as the MTCR and which are not easily produced by most states themselves.

Understanding whether technology will diffuse quickly on its own is important since proposals to control the spread of armed drones hinge on the idea that the spread of drones is not inexorable. If drone proliferation becomes easy and rampant, then trying to influence responsible drone exports would be not only futile but even counterproductive. In this scenario, the drone industry would be correct to say that if the United States does not supply or export drones, other states will, and the United States will lose out on market share.[18] Indeed, this is very much what happened to the satellite industry in the 1990s when Congress chose to restrict the export of satellites once it began considering them as a potential military tool. The US share of the satellite market dropped from 73% to 30% and the technology became ubiquitous when Europe branded its satellites as unconstrained by the type of regulations that had been put in place in the United States.[19] As this discussion suggests, there are reasons to believe that advanced armed drone technology will not be ubiquitous, in which case efforts to stem proliferation can be fruitful at least in terms of the supply side of the technology.

Q. Does the proliferation of drones present security risks?

The nature of the proliferation concern would depend on the type of drone in question. Advanced armed drones are likely to be destabilizing for regional and international security. As the UN Special Rapporteur for extrajudicial, summary or arbitrary executions noted, "drones make it not only physically easier to dispatch long-distance and targeted armed force, but the proliferation of drones may lower social barriers in society against the deployment of lethal force and result in attempts to weaken the relevant legal standards."[20] The report goes on to say that because the use of drones does not introduce casualties on the side using them, they will be used more readily.

If drones do lower the threshold for using force, then the states that acquire them will be more willing to use or threaten force than they might otherwise. They might take more cross-border, interstate actions with fewer reservations, which would be particularly destabilizing in areas that are already prone to distrust, such as the East and South China Seas. Similarly, the CIA reports that there are more than 430 bilateral maritime boundaries that are not governed by formal agreements. These boundaries, where the rules governing them are ambiguous, would be more susceptible to the use of armed drones, since states could literally "test the waters" with less risk than would be incurred with a manned equivalent.

A good example of the possible future of drone tactics and their destabilizing effects is the spate of Russian air incursions into NATO airspace in the Baltic Sea region. The *International Business Times* has written that "while the Russian patrols are regarded for now as routine, officials are sounding alarm that NATO has already registered 400 similar intercepts and the year (then 2014) has yet to end. Needless to say, the incursion spikes are directly connected with Moscow's soured relationship with the west."[21] If long-range drones are added to the mix, the number of incursions into NATO airspace could significantly escalate as the costs of incursion decrease for Russia.

Similarly, in 2015 tensions spiked around the India–Pakistani border after Pakistan's army shot down a drone that it claimed was spying, the allegation being that India was infiltrating Pakistani airspace near the Line of Control in Pakistan-occupied Kashmir.

The potentially destabilizing consequences could be more intense because of the unclear rules of engagement that attend the use of armed drones. Most states do not have clear operating procedures for drones entering their airspace. China, for example, is reported to have a policy of shooting down unannounced drones with surface-to-air missiles or jet fighters.[22] Iran is thought to have brought down drones in two cases, one a US RQ-170 surveillance drone in 2011, and the other an

Israeli surveillance drone over the Natanz enrichment site in 2014. The former is thought to have been taken down by an Iranian cyberwarfare unit.[23] The dilemma, as Panetta has put it, was this:

> was this a deliberate act of war by Iran or the foolish work of a rogue pilot? Without knowing the answer to that question, we also faced a second: should we fly the routine mission again—it occurred every few days—or call it off? If we did fly, and the drone was shot down, we'd be in an explosive situation with Iran. If we didn't, we'd effectively be acquiescing to Iran's unwarranted attack. The last thing we needed was for Iran to conclude that it could shoot at us with impunity.[24]

As these examples suggest, even the use of unmanned surveillance aircraft raise a number of uncertainties about how states use force, and the calculus about how other states might respond when confronting drones. Some states, such as China and Iran, might be less reluctant to shoot down drones. Complicating matters, as Panetta suggests, are that rules of engagement for how the country operating the drone responds in turn are currently ambiguous. On one hand, those countries would not be in a legitimate position to retaliate given that they would be or were violating another country's airspace, but on the other hand, in areas where territorial boundaries are less clear, the absence of clear rules of engagement is problematic. The international relations scholar Robert Jervis shows how a number of examples about decision-making under conditions of uncertainty explain how "people draw inferences from ambiguous evidence and, in turn, help explain many seemingly incomprehensible policies. They show how, when, and why highly intelligent and conscientious statesmen misperceive their environments in specific ways and reach inappropriate decisions."[25]

Where rules are unclear and misperceptions may already reside, the prospect for escalation becomes a concern. Indeed, that neither the United States nor Israel would retaliate in response to their drones being shot down is not obvious; either state might have done so, leading to the potential for escalation. Even the expectation that the United States or Israel would not retaliate could have the paradoxical effect of encouraging more aggressive stances from Iran. In this regard, the ambiguity about rules of engagement for cyberconflict mirrors that for drones. What constitutes an act of aggression? And what are the appropriate responses to those acts of aggression? The technology has led these policies and may create openings for miscommunication and ultimately conflict.

Another concern that intensifies this dynamic is the uncertainty, as the 2013 report notes, "about which States are developing and acquiring armed drones."[26] For states to be deterred from using force, they need to have as much information as possible about the force that would meet them in retaliation. States—and indeed nonstates—have been quite cagey about their capabilities, perhaps hoping that others will conclude that their own capabilities are more formidable than they actually are, essentially bluffing. This seems to have been the case with Hamas's drone in 2014, which proved hopeless against the Israeli Defense Force (IDF) air defenses. A number of countries tout their version of the American Predator—including China with its Pterodactyl and Turkey with the Anka. Turkish Aerospace Industries has remarked that "if you can't buy them, copy them," but how well-executed those copies are remains unclear.[27]

Beyond the context of changing how states engage in interstate conflict, the possession of armed drones might also change the way states use force at the intrastate level. For some of the same reasons that states find drones attractive in an interstate setting—primarily that they come at low risk and cost—they might be inclined to use them against perceived domestic enemies. Many of the countries that have or are pursuing armed drones, such as Russia, Pakistan, China, and Turkey, have opposition or insurgency movements that have challenged leaders' rule. Drones might provide attractive answers to these leaders, choosing to target insurgency or suspected terrorist networks with drones rather than ground forces or manned aircraft. Insurgents would most likely lack basic air defenses, and drones, with their precision and long loiter time, might be seen as being able to perform tasks that may otherwise be too risky.

In addition to the destabilization that could come from states acquiring armed drones, and the overall lack of solid intelligence on the lethality and strength of the fleet, comes the potential for destabilization from more specialized drones. Smaller, unarmed drones, if used together as a "swarm," could be reason for concern, as they can be used to overwhelm enemy air defenses. These might seem less advanced, but still they require significant engineering capabilities. Mechanical engineer Vijay Kumar characterized the problem: "these devices take hundreds of measurements each second, calculating their position in relation to each other, working cooperatively toward particular missions, and just as important, avoiding each other despite moving quickly and in tight formations."[28] Flying this many drones in formation would require sophisticated hardware and software that would be out of reach for many countries but possible and quite harmful for those who can acquire it.

Another type of swarming threat would come from "dirty drones" that could be armed with chemical agents such as sarin. The US military appears to be concerned about this and is soliciting technologies that can defend against these drones. Detecting these drones would present challenges for sensor systems such as Joint Surveillance Target Attack Radar System (JSTARS) that are typically oriented toward larger assets. The challenge for defense arises from being sensitive enough to detect micro-drones but not so sensitive that they detect everything that moves.

While there are a number of drone technologies that in and of themselves could present security risks, it is important to point out the potential security benefits that might arise from using drones. Surveillance and reconnaissance drones, in particular, may increase transparency in ways that could defuse tensions. Surveillance drones such as the Global Hawk, for example, might actually promote the kind of exchange of information and transparency that helps alleviate uncertainty on which the seeds of conflict might otherwise be sown. Drones are also being used in the service of homeland security to monitor borders and interdict drug producers and smugglers in countries ranging from Mexico to Bolivia to China. Indeed, since 2014, the Chinese government has been using drones in mountainous regions of the country to conduct anti-drug reconnaissance missions, a use of drones that follows how countries in Latin America have been using drones for surveillance for the last several years. Whether they instead contribute to escalation in areas that are crisis-prone such as East Asia remains to be seen. As mentioned previously, the lack of clear rules of engagement could prove fateful if even an unarmed drone crosses into another country's airspace without explicit permission.

Q. Could terrorists carry out a strike with drones?

On the one hand, lone-wolf terrorists already have a number of tools at their disposal for killing large numbers of individuals, including the rudimentary but quite lethal AK-47 that the alleged terrorist on the high-speed train from Amsterdam to Paris had planned to use to kill scores of people in a 2015 episode. These weapons are already available and can potentially be devastating. On the other hand, drones may be the perfect tools for terrorists. There are several features of drones that could make them conducive to terrorism.[29]

First, they offer flexibility in terms of launch sites, since small drones can be launched even by hand, which means they do not

require sophisticated ground stations. Similarly, their ability to loiter and wait for the appropriate time to strike offers strategic value
in terms of maximizing damage, essentially acting as airborne
improvised explosive devices (IEDs) that can seek out specific
high-value targets instead of hoping those targets will be in prox-
imity to a stationary explosive device.[30] Senator Dianne Feinstein
(D-CA) believes that, "in some respects, it's a perfect assassination
weapon. It can see from 17,000 to 20,000 ft. up in the air, it is very
precise, it can knock out a room in a building if it's armed, it's a
very dangerous weapon."[31] Even low-cost drones could be used
in a kamikaze style to target an individual or, if equipped with a
biological or a chemical agent, be quite disruptive.

Second, many air defense systems that could target larger
aircraft are likely to be unsuccessful against smaller drones. A
good example is a North Korean spy drone, which has a 5- to
6-foot wingspan and whose wreckage has been found repeatedly in South Korea. Analysis of the wreckage suggested that
drones had been able to cross into South Korean airspace for
a one-year time period, and revealed camera equipment that
had collected images of the Demilitarized Zone and the South
Korean president's office and residence. While these quite
rudimentary drones were fairly benign because of their low
payloads, one concern is whether they could be reconfigured
to carry nuclear or chemical devices. Moreover, the act of penetrating South Korean air defenses points to how these drones
could be used in larger numbers to swarm across the border
and do considerable collective impact. As defense analyst Van
Jackson put it in *Foreign Policy*, "it's the low-performance quali-
ties of North Korea's drones that enable them to evade South
Korean defenses, which are optimized for more traditional
threats from bigger, faster, higher-altitude aircraft."[32]

Third, while these small drones might not be a weapon of
mass destruction, they would certainly have an important
psychological impact, along the lines of a terrorist attack that
serves to unnerve the population. Indeed, in the case of the
North Korean drone, the fact that even a small system could

penetrate air defenses multiple times jarred the population. One Air Force colonel in Korea explained that this threat by North Korea took on high political salience for South Korean politicians who were trying to cultivate images as leaders who were attentive to the populace's security concerns. The idea of terrorism is to create psychological anxiety and in this sense even a hobbyist drone, despite its seemingly harmless design could terrorize a population whether unarmed or mounted with small amounts of a chemical or biological weapon.

Lastly, since individuals can buy personal drones inexpensively and easily online, the issue of ownership and attribution could be extremely difficult, making retaliation difficult and therefore doing little to deter an attack in the first place. Drone owners had not been required to register their aircraft, which made the issue of attribution—and retaliation and deterrence—virtually impossible. Even once the government requires registration, individuals could assemble their own drones that are not only not registered but also not bound by the type of "geofencing" that manufacturers have placed on some drones to prevent the drone from going near airports, for example. States could also plausibly deny involvement in a drone-related terrorist incident given that there would be no pilot implicated and the type of drone used might well not bear any markings or radio signature that identifies the sponsor. Thus, the factors that might deter individuals or groups from carrying out an attack—retaliation—might not be operative for drones.

Nonetheless, even state-sponsored terrorist groups are likely to find drones to have somewhat limited utility in a more conventional setting. The group Hezbollah has been sending drones into Israeli airspace for about a decade now but with limited success. In November 2004, Hezbollah piloted a drone into Israeli airspace, hovering over and observing the town of Nahariya for roughly 20 minutes before returning to its launch site in Lebanon. The next two attempts to send drones into

Israel, in April 2005 and August 2006, were intercepted by the Israeli military. Hezbollah stopped sending drones into Israel for six years, before picking up again in 2012. On October 6, 2012, Hezbollah sent an Iranian "Ayub" drone into Israel, seemingly sending it to the town of Dimona, the site of Israel's nuclear weapons complex. After shooting down the drone, Israeli military examined the wreckage and claimed that the drone had the capability of communicating information about the nuclear facility back to Hezbollah. Weeks later, a member of the Iranian parliament claimed that the nation had received images of Israeli nuclear facilities from the drone.[33]

In its summer 2014 conflict with Israel, Hamas also appeared to be interested in the psychological dividend of having drones, taking to Twitter to brag about having "armed drones." Israel, for its part, was unimpressed and ultimately shot down two of the drones, which appeared to be quite rudimentary and far from the advanced drones that the United States has been using for counterterrorism.[34] In the conflict with Hamas two years earlier, Israel reported that it had targeted a Hamas drone production facility. Persevering as though drones confer prestige, Hamas flew a drone in its December 2014 memorial to mark the group's 27th anniversary, prompting Israel to scramble warplanes, though the aircraft never crossed into Israeli airspace.[35]

Because of the potential limitations of drones in a conventional conflict the terrorist activity associated with drones is more likely to occur in a less conventional setting. For example, the type of lone wolves that carried out the hostage attack in Sydney, Australia in December 2014 or the Boston Marathon in April 2013 could find a drone well-suited to a terrorist attack, insofar as the aggressor could fly the drone remotely into a crowded area, maximizing damage, or at least maximizing psychological terror. Unfortunately, much as the non-drone terrorist strikes are difficult to guard against, those involving drones would also be quite complicated to defend against because drones are both small and also legally available for hobby and commercial uses, making the sight of a drone in an urban setting perhaps unusual but not necessarily alarming.

Q. What types of institutions are in place to deal with the proliferation of drones?

Currently, the MTCR controls the transfer of advanced drones. As mentioned earlier, the regime was created in 1987 as a nuclear nonproliferation arrangement designed to limit the spread of nuclear weapons delivery vehicles. The organization has questionable relevance because of the membership composition and rules. While the United States has generally adhered to the MTCR, the regime excludes the world's other key drone producers, including Israel, China, and Iran.

The discussion of drone proliferation should be taken in the context of which drone-producing countries are part of the MTCR and thus bound by MTCR guidelines. Members have all agreed that they will engage in consultation with other MTCR members before exporting anything on a list of items that has been deemed sensitive. Specifically, the organization has a strong presumption of denial when it comes to Category I drones, which the organization states should be exported rarely and conducted on a rare, case-by-case basis. Category II drones are thought to be of less concern from the standpoint of proliferation. "Other" refers to even less-sensitive drone technology that falls outside the purview of the MTCR, either technology demonstrators such as the nEUROn, made by a European consortium, or smaller drones that are considered fully exportable.

Table 3.1 is based on data collected by Lynn Davis and his colleagues from the Rand Corporation and categorizes the states thought to be developing Category I and II systems on the basis of their MTCR membership. The category that represents the greatest proliferation concern is the Category I-Not MTCR box, which includes China, India, Iran, Taiwan, and UAE.[36] In

Table 3.1 Countries' Drone Acquisition (Current and Planned) by MTCR Membership

	Category I	Category II	Other
MTCR Member	Russia Turkey United States	South Africa	France Germany Greece Italy South Korea Spain Sweden United Kingdom
Not MTCR Member	China India Iran Taiwan UAE	Israel Pakistan	Lebanon North Korea Switzerland Tunisia

Source: Davis et al. 2014, *Armed and Dangerous,* 9.

some senses, that category is somewhat misleading since it includes countries such as China that have already developed Category I systems, as well as countries such as India, which are in the initial stages of developing a stealthy unmanned combat aerial vehicle called the Aura.[37] Nonetheless, it illustrates the concern that many countries capable of producing this technology fall outside the MTCR altogether.

Even Category II systems are controlled by the MTCR for a reason, which is that they are seen as potentially playing a negative role in delivering weapons, their 186-mile range being long enough to inflict harm. As the table shows, a number of countries are capable of producing Category II systems but are not in the MTCR. In short, one concern with the MTCR is that it is a regulating agency that does not incorporate all of the countries producing drones, implying a major flaw in its institutional design. Even if it is not a legally binding treaty, which also raises a potential concern, the states that are members have generally adhered to the MTCR's guidelines, with countries such as the United States exporting Category I drones on a restrictive basis, denying requests from countries such as Pakistan, Turkey, and the UAE for such systems.[38]

Another proliferation concern having to do with the MTCR arises from the arbitrary threshold of its guidelines, which can present problems of false negatives, the technologies that are less restricted under the MTCR but could present proliferation problems, and false positives, those that are restricted that actually otherwise might have salutary impacts on regional security. First, with technology becoming lighter, a drone that is currently a Category I system could easily be converted into a Category II system that is less restricted by export controls. For example, General Atomics, which makes the Predator, has been flooded with international requests for the drone but has been held back by export restrictions. Instead, it created a version of the Predator that would more easily circumvent those restrictions, lowering the payload in part by integrating lower-end sensors and sidestepping weaponization. To be sure, this particular exportable version has end-user agreements that prevent weaponization or transfer to third parties, but studies of end-user certification in the context of international arms markets point to a number of problems when it comes to international verification—for example, forged certificates and increasingly global markets that challenge the traditional control systems.[39] Being able to sidestep the somewhat arbitrary Category I threshold and more freely export advanced drones could therefore have the effect of increasing the number of such drones in the international market and putting those drones in the hands of states that might not observe the end-user prohibitions against weaponization.

Second, an inverse problem associated with the MTCR is one that might be referred to as "false positives," which would include systems whose exports are prohibited under the MTCR but do not necessarily create security problems as a result of their proliferation. Global Hawk could fit under this heading. On the one hand, as one Air Force general cautioned,

Global Hawk could be seen as "ultra, ultra-long range cruise missiles."[40] It is in this spirit that talks with Japan about the proposed sale of Global Hawks had been sensitive. On the other hand, the Global Hawk's surveillance capability could actually create much-needed transparency in regions such as East Asia, where tactical miscalculations resulting from inadequate data can result in escalating conflict. It was with these ambitions in mind that the United States arranged a sale of a European variant of the Global Hawk, the Euro Hawk, to Germany and negotiated a proposed sale of Global Hawks to South Korea, which had required that South Korea reduce its commitments to the MTCR. *Jane's Defense Weekly* reported that the 2012 deal had "relaxed" South Korea's commitments to the MTCR.[41]

As this discussion implies, the MTCR is an imperfect proliferation measure for a technology that has evolved in ways that were not envisioned at its inception in 1987. In light of the existence of drone producers outside of the MTCR, some scholars have proposed a drone proliferation organization that would address the regulation gap between member countries in the MTCR and those outside of its jurisdiction. Philosopher Allen Buchanan and political scientist Robert Keohane have advocated an informal regime that promotes accountability in drone strikes. Before an attack takes place they propose "requiring that states specify appropriate procedures in their decision-making process for all drone strikes," and, after a drone attack, that states must make "public justifications for specific strikes."[42] Such a system acknowledges that strikes via drone are qualitatively different from F-16 strikes in that they tend to be able to be conducted covertly and therefore are beyond the traditional umbrella of international law. The regime would bring these strikes out of the covert world and require more transparency in the targeting process.

Other proposals acknowledge and seek to remedy deficiencies in the MTCR's regulations, particularly, that the countries seeking to export or import drones are often outside the purview of the MTCR, that the export thresholds are arbitrary and easily sidestepped, and that many states outside the MTCR stand to gain financially from drone exports, including China and Israel. One idea from scholars at the Council on Foreign Relations is to create a new and enhanced drone regime that includes the states outside the MTCR and seeks to regulate the exports of armed-capable drones. Its membership would go beyond the current MTCR, which could be tricky because it would bring in countries that are developing or exporting Category I systems and otherwise benefit from those exports. To generate support, the US would have to make some concessions, for example, being more forthcoming about how it uses drones and exchange its transparency for broader buy-in of the enhanced drone regime.[43]

In addition to the MTCR, the United Nations currently has in place two Special Rapporteurs—one on counterterrorism and human rights and another on extrajudicial, summary, and arbitrary executions—who are meant to monitor and report on the use of drones. Both act as watchdogs of how drones are used in conflict. The former, for example, is charged with ensuring that the promotion and protection of human rights and fundamental freedoms are not violated during counterterrorism activities, with a mandate established by the Commission on Human Rights in 2005. Ben Emmerson assumed the post of Special Rapporteur in 2011 and in 2014 reported on reductions in the rate of civilian casualties in Pakistan. Yet he also acknowledged that that between 24 and 71 civilians were killed in Yemen between 2009 and 2013 and concurred that the European Union's condemnation of strikes outside a declared war raised serious concerns about the legality of these strikes under international law. Finally, he drew attention to the continuing opaqueness in terms of the United States' specific strikes, specifically, which civilian casualties are sustained, how and why—even in the context of ongoing conflicts, such as those in Afghanistan.[44]

As Emmerson's report indicated, the findings are intended to be read in tandem with that of the investigation of the Special

Rapporteur on extrajudicial, summary or arbitrary executions, whose 2013 report notes that drones themselves are not illegal but "can make it easier for States to deploy deadly and targeted force on the territories of other States." The report added that the broad justifications deployed to legitimize drone strikes run the risk of undermining international legal limits to the use of force. The report also foreshadows the future landscape, which consists of a proliferation of multiple drones by states and nonstates against a backdrop of more actors using force less discriminately. Since the use of the technology means no casualties by the actor that uses drones, the international community should become more attentive in scrutinizing states' drone strikes and providing clarity on the conditions under which self-defense is being invoked, including more transparency on targeting, civilian impact, and violations prompting the use of drone strikes.[45]

Other than through multilateral institutions, the other way to affect the future acquisition or use of armed drones is through state practice. The state that has been most involved in drone technology has been the United States; this gives it the potential to help establish legal precedents, not just in terms of the sale of armed drones but also in how drones are used in conflict. To this end, the United States has been urged by critics to clarify certain aspects of its drone program, including what it defines as "imminence," the actual conditions that it considers capture not to be feasible—meaning that killing is warranted—and criteria for targeting.[46]

Although the preceding discussion emphasized the international regulation of armed drones, the prospect of ubiquity of even smaller-scale drones that are largely unregulated presents potentially enormous security threats. As the January 2015 landing of a drone on the White House lawn served to illustrate, these devices are seemingly boundless, and certainly not bound by the same impediments—such as a fence—that ground threats would be. The US Department of Homeland Security has investigated how smaller drones could be used to catastrophic effect. As they concluded, a standard civilian drone is able to carry three pounds of explosives, which would certainly be disruptive.[47] Along similar lines, a drone carrying six pounds of methamphetamine in Mexico and destined for the United States crashed on the US border, but in so doing illustrated the way borders become far more permissive when a vehicle is an aerial drone. The drones that international traffickers repurpose as so-called blind mules to transport drugs across borders provide yet another way to circumvent more established law enforcement boundaries. The drones are not themselves illegal but of course trafficking is illegal and the third-party GPS autopilot device means that law enforcement cannot track even crashed drones back to the operator.[48] As these examples illustrate, states are increasingly aware of the threats posed by the type of drone that has flown under the radar of international regulations but have yet to come up with effective countermeasures, though these are certainly under consideration.

4

DRONES FOR THE GROUND AND SEA

Until this point, the discussion has focused on drones as unmanned *aerial* technology. This is consistent with how the term "drone" is conventionally used. It is also consistent with the way many countries have channeled their unmanned resources. The United States' unmanned systems funding shows that the vast majority of resources are dedicated to aerial systems. As Table 4.1 shows almost 91% of the US budget for unmanned systems for the years 2014–2018 are planned for aerial systems. Nonetheless, under the broad heading of unmanned systems and automation, it is worth considering two other domains: ground and sea and this chapter surveys both.

Q. What types of unmanned technologies exist for ground environments?

Many of the technologies associated with ground environments follow closely with the logic behind using unmanned aerial vehicles, which is to carry out tasks that would be too dangerous or arduous for troops on the ground. In a military context, one of the most significant threats posed to ground forces are ambushes. Between 2003 and 2007, ambushes killed more than 3,000 American soldiers in Iraq and Afghanistan. Aerial-based surveillance and reconnaissance platforms

Table 4.1 United States Department of Defense Unmanned Systems Funding ($ Million)

Year	Air	Ground	Sea	Total
2014	3775.9	13.0	330.3	4119.1
2015	4819.4	47.0	409.8	5276.2
2016	4467.6	44.3	408.6	4920.5
2017	4217.0	52.7	429.7	4700.4
2018	4419.3	66.0	381.8	4867.1
Total across years	**21,699.1**	**223.9**	**1960.2**	**23,883.2**

Source: *Unmanned Systems Integrated Roadmap FY2013–2038.*

can be particularly helpful in identifying these threats. One unmanned ground vehicle (UGV), the PackBot, which is about the size of a small suitcase, works alongside soldiers to conduct surveillance. In a military setting this allows the vehicle to identify and dispose of explosives, and to check for the use of chemical agents. In a civilian context the PackBot can patrol public settings, using real-time video, audio, and sensor data to assess potential public threats.[1] Most recently, PackBots were used in this manner during the 2014 World Cup in Brazil to ensure the public's safety throughout the event.[2]

A number of UGVs have come to serve a similar function in terms of surveillance and reconnaissance. Indeed, the origins of unmanned ground systems came from the British Ministry of Defense Explosive Ordnance Disposal (EOD) team, which was tasked with defusing terrorist bombs in the 1970s. UGVs are now routinely used for identifying and defusing improvised explosive devices (IEDs). As Lieutenant Colonel Arnald Thomas notes, UGVs "avoid human endurance constraints." Humans need rest and have limited attention, two limitations that do not arise in the context of an unmanned vehicle.[3] UGVs are also preferable to using bomb-sniffing dogs and therefore are frequently deployed with EOD teams as an alternative to them.

To serve these functions, a UGV often has instruments designed to observe its environment, and will use the information it gathers to make decisions independently, or it will relay the data it collects to a human operator who controls the vehicle remotely. Lockheed Martin and the US Army Tank Automotive Research, Development and Engineering Center have partnered together in an attempt to develop self-driving technology that can be installed in the military's vehicles. This would allow supply vehicles to be operated remotely, reducing the likelihood of casualties from ambushes.

One of the most widely used UGVs is the TALON, whose main purpose is bomb disposal but also surveillance of enemy territory, which helps anticipate and avoid ambushes or explosions. Developed by the Army's EOD Technology Directorate, TALON was involved in combat operations in Bosnia in 2000, Afghanistan in 2002, and Iraq throughout the war. It is reported to be remarkably hardy, being all-weather, capable of operating day and night, and amphibious up to a 100-ft. depth. QinetiQ, which makes TALON robots, advertises the hardiness of the technology by reporting that a TALON was "blown off the roof of a Humvee in Iraq while the Humvee was crossing a bridge over a river. TALON flew off the bridge and plunged into the river below. Soldiers later used its operator control unit to drive the robot back out of the river and up onto the bank so they could retrieve it."[4] Variations of TALON include the TALON HAZMAT, which uses sensors to test for chemicals, gas, and radiological threats. TALON HAZMAT sends that information back to its controller in real time. It is ideal for scouting out situations in a potentially hazardous environment.

In addition to surveillance and reconnaissance, UGVs can also circumvent threats that humans face in the supply and transportation of materials in a combat zone. The Army has worked to develop an unmanned transport system that is essentially an unmanned convoy. In a 2014 demonstration, the Army operated driverless vehicles that navigated both rural and urban courses, various traffic patterns, and pedestrians, all while keeping to its preprogrammed itinerary. As the head of the science and technology at the Army Capabilities Integration Center indicated, "We're not looking to replace soldiers with robots. It's about augmenting and increasing capability," including "the giant logistics tail" that can be vulnerable to attack.[5]

While these technologies are characterized by a primarily defensive capability, other technologies foreshadow the type of strike capability that has come to be used on aerial drones. The Special Weapons Observation Reconnaissance Detection System (SWORDS) builds on the idea of the TALON in that it is remotely operated and durable to damage and water, but is also equipped with several types of weapons, including a grenade launcher or machine gun. *Time* magazine reported in 2004 that SWORDS was one of the world's most amazing inventions. In 2007 three SWORDS units, each armed with a machine gun, were deployed to Iraq. Although their weapons have never been used, their deployment marked the first time that robots carried guns into battle (albeit without firing a shot). Rumors swirled about why the SWORDS system did not fire a shot, and after speculation that the system had shot errant bullets, the contractor suggested that the Army preemptively decided not to use the system. An Army program manager's explanation for the SWORDS's removal—"once you've done something that's really bad, it can take 10 to 20 years to try it again"—suggests that the military was being cautious with the deployment of the new technology, seeking to avoid a public relations debacle that could set the technology back decades.[6]

The move to develop an unmanned ground combat vehicle has proven to be challenging. The ground combat vehicle infantry carrier, intended to replace the Bradley fighting vehicle in the 2020s, was cancelled. Nonetheless, the Army is looking to become leaner and meaner, which likely means adopting unmanned technologies that could allow it to reduce combat teams and rely more on robotics. With this goal in mind, the Army issued a document that emphasized a "blue-sky" approach to spark big thinking about the future.[7] In other words, the sky should be the limit when it comes to thinking about the future of unmanned ground technologies.

Q. What is the state of proliferation in terms of unmanned ground technologies?

The UGV market is set to grow over fivefold over the next five years, from about $1.51 billion in 2014 to $8.26 billion by 2020. Countries are increasingly recognizing advantages in terms of troop safety, whether to do surveillance and reconnaissance before entering an area, for example, spotting snipers or removing IEDs.[8] The United States is the largest user of UGVs, owning roughly 45% of the UGVs in the world. The United Kingdom, Canada, France, and Germany are the next biggest users, all operating between 5% and 8% of existing UGVs. Israel, Australia, Switzerland, and Sweden each own approximately 3% of the UGVs in the world. The rest of the world commands roughly 17% of the world's UGV market, including Russia, which is increasingly interested in combat robots.[9] Figure 4.1 summarizes the market share by major country.

Even though the market in Europe, the continent with the second-largest UGV share after North America, is growing, it is doing so fairly slowly. The market, according to a major industry analysis, "has remained niche," in part because defense budgets have been shrinking, which means states can afford fewer numbers of a particular technology, increasing unit costs, making the technology less affordable, and so on.[10] Within Europe, the United Kingdom has been active in the development of modern UGVs, mostly for use in IED detection, engineering, and surveillance/reconnaissance. The Terrier Unmanned/Manned Combat Engineer Vehicle, for example, is able to operate in either manned or unmanned configuration, conducting route clearance even at night, as it is equipped with five cameras and thermal imaging technology

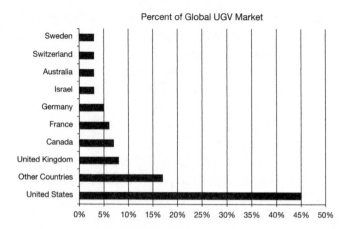

Figure 4.1 Share of World UGV Market by Country
Source: Association for Unmanned Vehicle Systems International.

that is used for surveillance. While mostly used in this capacity as route clearance, it is also used for transport and can even be equipped with a general-purpose machine gun and smoke grenade launcher for combat operations.

As with aerial drones, Israel has also very much been at the vanguard of UGVs, using them for reconnaissance, remote-controlled weapons, IED detection/disposal, and border surveillance. The Israeli Defense Force (IDF) justifies its investment in the technology in the following way: "Major threats are evolving on Israel's borders every day. . . . The superiority of Israel's technology is its greatest deterrent against these threats. Among its finest tools are UGVs, which could redefine Israel's capabilities in the near future."[11]

One of their primary systems is the Guardium, whose development began as an initiative of the IDF in 2008—a partnership between Israel Aerospace Industries and Elbit Industries. Originally meant to carry out reconnaissance and weapons operation, it became "one of the first regularly operating unmanned security vehicles in the world."[12] The Guardium MK III is fully autonomous, reportedly "creates deterrence by rapid closure of the sensor-to-shooter loop, identifies and classifies hostile activity, gives advance warning to military forces, and provides a threat response—all without endangering personnel."[13] With technology developing so quickly, the Guardium is being phased out for a new technology, called the Border Protector or Border Defender, which is intended to monitor the Gaza border with its cameras, operated by soldiers located long distances from the vehicle.

The next generation of UGVs to be deployed by the IDF is called the Loyal Partner. This iteration is an armored carrier, much like a Humvee, that can carry weapons and other equipment to deployed soldiers while also conducting surveillance. Also in the repertoire will be backpack-carried UGVs called Carrier Robots that "will do things that no human can, such as mapping entire buildings and terror tunnels," a term Israel uses to refer to the tunnels between Israel and its neighbors that traffic in weapons and terrorists.[14] The technology, as with unmanned technologies in general, will be able to overcome the limitations of humans. Whereas humans need rest and sleep, the unmanned counterparts can operate for hours and hours without a break. Moreover, the value of a human life is higher than that of a robot, which is more expendable and can therefore accept more risk in terms of engaging in urban conflict, encountering enemy fire, or even breathing in the tunnels.

Russia also holds a keen interest in developing UGVs not only for surveillance and reconnaissance but also to fire munitions. *Popular Mechanics* put it succinctly when it reported that Russia wants "fighting robots, and lots of them."[15] The versions in development are semiautonomous; however, Russia hopes to develop an autonomous version in the future. One type of system is a mobile shock-reconnaissance robotics system, which was tested and approved in April 2014. The system will be deployed to secure Russian missile sites. It will be operated from a remote site through a wireless connection. Russia's future goals include an autonomous artificial intelligence system that could be preprogrammed to carry out a wide range of activities, from patrol and reconnaissance missions to the destruction of targets, to providing security for those individuals protecting the missile sites.

Russia's vision for armed unmanned systems appears to be ambitious. While the United States has been cautious about deploying UGVs that fire weapons, Russia seems to be moving more aggressively in this direction. Russia anticipates using one robot to replace what today requires five to ten soldiers. One version of this technology is the Wolf-2, which is about the size of a Jeep, is amphibious, and can fire at targets with dual machine guns. Russia also has the Strelok, "Sharpshooter," which kicks down doors, climbs stairs, and is armed with a Kalashnikov; and the Metalliste, which is a six-wheeler with a silenced submachine gun. Despite these developments, *The Robot Report* concludes that "Russians have a lot of catching up to do when it comes to sophisticated fighting robots," having fallen far behind the Israelis and Americans in development.[16]

Following in the footsteps of the states seeking unmanned technology for locating and defusing IEDs, India has developed Daksh, an electrically-powered, remote-controlled unmanned ground robot that is intended to identify and defuse all types of hazardous objects, primarily IEDs. It can also climb stairs, carry relatively heavy hazardous objects, and operate for three hours on a full charge. The first delivery of five Dakshs took place in December 2011 and was India's first indigenously developed robot, beating out the British equivalent that the Indian Army also tested. A new version as of September 2015 is three times faster and has the ability to survey areas contaminated by nuclear, biological, or chemical exposure, and a mounted weapon.[17] India is also looking into unmanned ground combat vehicles that could perform counterinsurgency operations, recover hostages, or disrupt indoor hostage situations, which otherwise would put soldiers at risk, while also mounting a light machine gun or grenade launcher. In short, India has been moving quickly in developing homegrown UGVs.

China is also venturing into the development of UGVs but is estimated to be about five years behind the United States and Israel. China seems to have identified unmanned ground technology as the wave of the future, however, and has made a number of major pronouncements in 2014 about future plans. According to an officer in the People's Liberation Army, "unmanned ground vehicles will play a very important role in future ground combat. Realizing that, we have begun to explore how to refit our armored vehicles into unmanned ones."[18] Another officer, the president of the PLA Academy of Armored Forces Engineering in Beijing, said that "though we have yet to develop unmanned tanks, I think it is an irreversible trend that computers will gradually replace humans to control those fighting machines." In June 2014, China North Industries Group, a major defense firm, created China's first research center for developing UGVs.[19] The Deputy Director of the Center cited the United States' success with UGVs in Iraq and Afghanistan as a motivation behind developing their own systems that can carry out tasks more safely and remotely.

A number of other countries are developing technologies similar to those described above. Many of these are based in Canada and the European Union, with some exceptions such as the South African Testudo Unmanned Ground Robot, which can climb stairs, is capable of performing civil and military missions, such as explosives disposal and reconnaissance, and has a top speed of 3.7 mph and endurance of 6 hours with one charge. The vehicle is meant for both military missions such as explosives disposal, reconnaissance, and mine surveying and also civilian missions such as search and rescue.

In sum, despite the fact that only a couple of states have significant UGV programs, a number of others are investing more resources in future development. Meanwhile, the unmanned ground combat vehicles that the United States developed in the mid-2000s have never seen fielded use due to an abundance of caution about the unintended operational consequences. Whether the countries that are developing these technologies will follow suit by exercising comparable caution, or whether the United States is just waiting to use its technologies or to further develop and test its fleet, remains to be seen.

Q. Are unmanned ground technologies likely to be game changers?

Although these technologies serve important functions in terms of minimizing exposure to threats that ground troops would otherwise face, there are more natural limitations to the use of these technologies than there are to aerial drones. As the discussion above indicates, the Army itself is ambivalent about next-generation vehicles, having cancelled not just the unmanned Bradley replacement vehicle but also the Future Combat System (FCS), which had planned to integrate unmanned ground systems with aerial drones; together, these two cancellations undermined progress toward ground-based unmanned systems. Indeed, unmanned systems have had nowhere near the operational impact on the ground as they have in the air.

Beyond the fact that developments have lagged behind those in the Air Force, another reason why the technologies have not been transformative is that many appear to be more defense-oriented, unlike aerial drones that have a clear offensive mission of striking targets. Moreover, although particular UGVs are indispensible in terms of IED detonation, many others have operational limitations. For example, the ground is typically densely populated with obstacles that confound the unmanned system's ability to navigate, let alone survive against enemy fire. These vehicles would likely be slow moving, making them vulnerable to attack. Additionally, the more offensively minded they would be, the larger, more lumbering, more visible, and therefore more vulnerable they would be vis-à-vis the adversary. Indoor settings might be less densely populated or vulnerable but because hallways often block radio signals, unmanned vehicles are unable to move easily within walled structures, making employment in particular urban environments difficult. This limitation makes them better suited to ascertain the security of outside spaces, such as a courtyard.

Yet another related limitation is the set of tradeoffs involving sensors, space, and weight such that improvements along one parameter limit the advantages along another. Any useful unmanned ground device would require not only night vision but also infrared for seeing through smoke. These sensors, however, would add weight and necessitate a large battery. The added capabilities carry a tradeoff in terms of making the vehicle more sizeable, limiting its range (portability), again making it more visible.[20]

Despite having some limitations, UGVs have significantly changed the explosive ordnance disposal missions conducted by national armed forces by limiting risks for one of the most dangerous components of the military. UGVs are particularly well-positioned to have an important impact in certain regions with heavily militarized borders such as the Korean Peninsula, Indian subcontinent, and the Middle East. Israel has been the most successful in making sophisticated UGVs operational in the past decade including unmanned ground combat vehicles, which could impact relations with neighbors and adversaries. For example, the kidnapping of Israeli soldier Gilad Shalit during a 2006 cross-border raid would not have occurred if Israel had replaced human troops with UGVs. Beyond this, civilians in Israeli border towns live in fear of Hamas raids and terrorist attacks from underground tunnels during periods of conflict, and UGVs could help enhance security in and around the tunnels. India would be able to take many lessons from Israel's development of UGVs because it too experiences insecurity along the Line of Control (LoC) with Pakistan in the region of Kashmir, mostly arising from ceasefire violations. With UGVs in place along the border, India could avert these violations, which have become a major source of tension between the two nuclear-armed neighbors. It would also help avoid situations like the one in January 2013, when two Indian soldiers in a border patrol were killed, and one was beheaded, thus leading to a major breakdown of diplomatic relations between the two states, and an escalation of firing along the LoC as well.[21] They could also be useful for border patrol and the manning of outposts not just in sensitive areas but also the Siachen glacier, where there are extreme weather conditions.

For countries such as Israel and India, the technologies also offer a more cost-effective way of monitoring their borders. These countries spend considerable amounts of resources protecting their borders, and unmanned systems would aid in identifying potential border incursions without the dull, dirty, and dangerous consequences that can come with the traditional mechanisms of border patrol. Of course, unmanned technologies also lower the cost of taking border patrol missions too far by venturing into another country's territory, analogous to the dynamic involving aerial drones. This possibility could have negative consequences, serving to inflame bilateral relations between neighboring states. Indeed, Israel's reported shoot-down of a Syrian drone that crossed into disputed territory of the Golan Heights intensified already-fraught relations between the two countries. This action contributed to a sense of tit-for-tat retaliation, which had the potential to destabilize the buffer zone of the Golan Heights.[22] A similar dynamic could play out with UGVs, with countries taking liberties that they might not if manned alternatives were deployed, causing border transgressions that only serve to intensify rather than defuse tensions.

Q. What is the status of unmanned technology for maritime systems?

Naval systems have evolved in similar ways to ground and aerial systems, starting with surveillance and reconnaissance missions and evolving to technologies that can detect mines and carry out strike missions. The technology is divided into unmanned underwater vehicles (UUVs), unmanned surface vehicles (USVs), and unmanned aerial vehicles that are integrated into aircraft carrier operations. This section examines these three categories of naval systems, focusing mostly on the use of UUVs and UAVs for maritime purposes since the development of USVs has been relatively slow by comparison. The number of air and sea vehicles is extensive and growing, so a comprehensive survey is not yet possible; this section therefore speaks to illustrative examples of how both are being developed.

Mines have long been the bane of navy ships; mines have damaged or sunk US Navy ships at four times the rate of any other form of attack. They have been a major threat in every major conflict since the Civil War. Mines tend to be a popular instrument of war since a $10,000 sea mine can sink a ship worth more than $1 billion, not to mention the human casualties that can result in the process.[23] Against the backdrop of this asymmetric threat, the prospect of UUVs is an attractive way to defend against the potential for destructive mines.

Indeed, early versions of unmanned naval systems were platforms dedicated expressly for demining. As the Naval Special Clearance Team program office notes about unmanned undersea vehicles' utility in Operation Iraqi Freedom, these "gadgets were the main workhorses of the mine clearing effort . . . if one got blown up in the process, the relatively cheap price meant it would be no big deal."[24] Military analysts have observed that such technologies could also defang Iran's efforts to mine the Strait of Hormuz as a way to prevent oil tankers from transporting oil, thus driving up prices. Its undeclared mining of the strait in the 1980s would therefore have been less plausible in an era of UUVs. Indeed, in 2012 the United States sent several SeaFox vehicles to do just that: detect and destroy any mines that would help Iran close the Strait. Launched from helicopters or rubber boats, the SeaFox is "on what amounts to a suicide mission" when it destroys a mine, in that it too is destroyed. Of course, this also implies that it shreds the $100,000 investment in each vehicle as well.[25]

There are a number of UUVs under development, most of which are in the area of intelligence, surveillance, and reconnaissance. One line of development seeks to mimic the movements of sea creatures in ways that could be useful for stealthy surveillance. The US Navy has a line of underwater drones, the GhostSwimmer, which can mimic jellyfish, eels, and the dorsal fin of a shark. The program is part of a larger program called Silent Nemo that seeks to bring new technologies into military platforms.

In terms of unmanned surface vessels (USVs), developments have been slower.[26] Current prototypes still require considerable manpower even for basic collision avoidance, which means having considerable bandwidth and either a manned platform or ground control station in the vicinity. The United States developed the Spartan Scout USV as a concept demonstration in 2002, and is a sensor and weapons system mounted onto an inflatable boat and used for demining or firing against small boats. Its main virtue is to provide a way of patrolling the seas without necessarily needing to put humans in harm's way, or to run into the limitations imposed by the need for rest. Though still a demonstration, its prototype was used in the Persian Gulf for harbor surveillance.[27] Singapore's Navy, which played a role in the initial development of the Scout, launched their own fleet of the USVs in 2005, primarily as a way to battle maritime piracy.[28] In 2010, Zyvex Marine completed development on a more advanced USV called the Piranha, made out of nanomaterials. The Piranha is made of nano-enhanced carbon fiber which is lighter than either fiberglass or aluminum, leading to fuel savings of 75% compared to traditional vessels, and is designed for harbor patrol and anti-piracy operations.[29]

The next frontier with these developments is in automation. In 2011, the Pentagon had made autonomy one of the military's major priorities, but has found itself further behind than it would like, with many objectives still aspirational. For example, a program officer in the Office of Naval Research suggested that in terms of autonomous decision-making on USVs, engineers still needed to develop better situational awareness, efficient algorithms for dealing with competing mission objectives, collective decision-making across unmanned platforms, network sensor fusion, detection of maritime hazards, and effective collision avoidance.[30]

Beyond these technical challenges lies the basic issue of trust in the system. Commanders must have confidence in the ability of the unmanned system to operate in predictable ways. In other words, the operator needs to have had enough interactions with the system to know that when he or she requests the system to do a task, it will do exactly what was requested, instead of having a mind of its own and acting in errant ways. For the time being, the Navy plans to employ a "human oversight mode" to guard against the unintended or unwanted outcomes of autonomous systems, such as collisions.

For one of the newest type of USVs, collision has been less important since the vehicle is a swarm boat whose purpose, in a sense, is to engage in just that: collision with a potentially hostile vessel such as the type that targeted the USS *Cole* in 2000, killing 17 sailors. In one test of swarming technology, a simulated enemy boat approached a convoy, and the human controller ordered five of the USVs to swarm the enemy vessel, leaving the other eight to continue escorting the manned ship. After the order, the five USVs, using a combination of sensor data and planned routes, each plotted their own course to the enemy ship, sharing information with each other and coordinating along the way.[31] Once the USVs had swarmed the "enemy" vessel, the simulation was stopped. The next step in development is to program the ships with rules of engagement, so that they autonomously target enemy combatants, ensuring that they avoid targeting allies or noncombatant ships. This is particularly important because in a war zone enemies often attempt to jam transmissions between the ships and their operators. A single operator would be in charge of orchestrating up to 30 USVs, unlike Predator pilots, who operate in a one-to-one ratio. The biggest obstacle may be the logistics of aiming and firing the weapons on each USV. A single operator could not possibly aim and fire machine guns from 30 different USVs, requiring the targeting and firing processes to be automated. One possibility is that humans will designate the target but the USVs will aim and fire autonomously. This kind of automation could eventually make these weapons safer than what the Navy currently uses. Whereas human operators are affected by the stress of battle or can become battle-weary, increasing the propensity for operator error, an automated weapon would be less prone to such impediments.

In terms of unmanned naval aviation, development dates back at least to the Pioneer. Launched by rocket-assisted takeoff or pneumatic rails, the Pioneer was later recovered at sea or in a landing field. The Navy, the Marines, and the Army have flown Pioneers in every military intervention since 1986, including more than 300 combat reconnaissance missions in the 1991 Gulf War, in which some Iraqis allegedly surrendered on the basis of the buzzing "vultures" overhead.[32]

More advanced carrier-based aerial systems are still in development. In July 2013, the United States Navy made history by landing a drone on the deck of a carrier, the USS *George HW Bush*, off Virginia. The aircraft was the X-47B, the Unmanned Combat Air System (UCAS), which is an experimental vehicle that has a range of 2,000 nautical miles and can fly at 40,000 ft.[33] It was the first pilotless aircraft to land on a carrier. About a year later, in August 2014, the UCAS landed within 90 seconds of the F/A-18E Super Hornet. The two aircraft achieved the Navy's goal of taking off and landing in close succession.

The UCAS is intended to be the prototype for the Navy's Unmanned Carrier-Launched Airborne Surveillance and Strike (UCLASS) program intended to be used for reconnaissance and precision strikes. The UCLASS program has had four different competing designs from Northrop Grumman, Lockheed Martin, Boeing, and General Atomics. The program has sparked some controversy over how it will be overseen. In late 2013, the Government Accountability Office issued a report calling for greater oversight of the program, arguing that the Navy was moving forward with the program in a way that made it difficult for Congress to hold them accountable for adhering to their planned schedule, costs, and capabilities.

While the US Navy is in the early stages of determining the requirements for the future UCLASS, internal divisions have delayed the request for proposal. Some constituencies believe that the platform should be ambitious and provide long-range surveillance and strike capabilities, along with some stealth. Another camp has a more modest vision, producing a system more quickly, even if it is less capable. In the meantime, the divide has led to the UCLASS at least temporarily losing funding out of concern that the vehicle would not be sufficiently stealthy, survivable, or potent in terms of payload. Yet the Navy still reports that it will field the UCLASS by 2020.[34]

Overall, the Navy sees unmanned systems as the way of the future, not only because of the upside in terms of capability and risk avoidance, but also because they could be cost-effective in tight fiscal environments. The size of vessels being considered for unmanned functions tends to be fairly small compared to manned vessels, even though they tend to have larger payload capacities and longer ranges in part because they free up space and weight by not having humans on board. Taken together, the prospect for cost savings may be considerable, and the Navy is pushing for more unmanned systems for the future. For example, the Navy has more recently modified the Israeli-made Protector platform, a USV intended to be used for anti-piracy missions or surveillance. In 2012, it conducted live-fire tests of the Protector, the first time it had fired missiles from the unmanned vehicle, with hopes of more tests before deciding to go ahead and add to its flotilla of unmanned assets.

Q. What is the state of proliferation in terms of unmanned technologies related to maritime environments?

The nonproliferation regime that deals with limiting the transfer of aerial vehicles would naturally include airborne systems such as the Navy's UCLASS, much as it includes a Predator or Reaper. They just happen to take off and land from an aircraft carrier, but the spirit of their use would fall under a similar heading of being able to serve as a nuclear delivery vehicle, much as the Missile Technology Control Regime (MTCR) had envisioned a cruise missile or drone to be capable of doing. These technologies could extend the range and lower the threshold for lethal force in ways discussed for drones in the sections above insofar as they would limit the risk to the actors using them compared to a manned equivalent, whose risk would give states pause before deploying them. There is no institutional nonproliferation equivalent for actual UUVs. Given that unmanned systems would confer a number of advantages, including sidestepping the human limits imposed by tasks that are dull, dirty, or dangerous, it is not surprising that other countries are trying to buy into the unmanned industry. The market for UUVs is expected to be $2 billion by 2020, far less than aerial vehicles, but many countries are joining the action.[35]

Similar to UGV proliferation, the United States, the United Kingdom, and Israel remain at the forefront of unmanned technologies related to maritime environments. Unlike UGV proliferation, however, the gap between the top three and the rest is not very large, as all states struggle to shift from relatively simple countermine/antisubmarine reconnaissance vessels to USVs/UUVs with enough firepower to defend fleets and launch offensive operations if needed.

As with unmanned aerial and ground vehicles, Israel has long been a leader in unmanned underwater and surface vehicles. As one observer has suggested, Israel has been "more agile in its thinking about how to deploy unmanned systems than were larger nations' militaries. Israel cannot support the cost of a large standing force, but its small military has major mission requirements and must maximize how it uses unmanned systems."[36] Much as it was at the forefront of unmanned systems in the 1970s and 1980s, it was an early developer of many "Protector" vessels that are unmanned and can sail unthreatened by potential terrorist attacks. The Protector approaches suspicious vehicles as the initial contact rather than a ship that is manned. The Protector has a number of sensors and cameras to meet this objective and newer systems have sensors that can anticipate and reorient in response to the next wave. Other variants are involved in demining activities, providing intelligence, and even shooting at targets.

Israel is currently seeking to develop a submarine drone that can conduct minesweeping operations that does not create risks to human lives in the process. Israel's aeronautics director for the next generation of weaponry compared the task of demining to "looking for a needle in a haystack. These are sophisticated mines, which activate themselves and explode at the acoustic signal of the engines of a ship passing overhead, changes in water pressure when a ship passes overhead, or magnetic mines, which attach to any metal ship."[37] Alternatively, mines might not be sophisticated but rather simply hard to see amidst all the debris in the ocean. Absent mine-clearing activities, ships are unable to pass through an area, effectively creating a blockade. Unmanned technologies are well-suited to identifying and clearing area—and at no risk to human lives—allowing ships to proceed safely. While Israel already uses unmanned submersibles, these vehicles are short-range and therefore limited. Automation of these systems would create the virtues of unmanned systems while offering longer-range prospects for minesweeping.

The British have long been using UUVs for demining. In particular, the Royal Navy has used these to prevent Iran from introducing mines in areas like the Strait of Hormuz, an important shipping lane, and has considered whether using these vessels for antipiracy missions off the Horn of Africa. The United Kingdom's Ministry of Defence has looked favorably upon these successes and has asked the defense industry to develop drones that can "provide greater support to maritime operations such as mine countermeasures, anti-submarine warfare, and missile defence ... innovation in maritime technology, including unmanned systems, will make it possible for UK armed forces to continue to use the sea with security and persistence." These systems include the UUVs, USVs, and unmanned air vehicles launched from ships. The Ministry believes that these unmanned technologies can address the problems of what they refer to as "dirty, dangerous and repetitive" jobs in ways that protect human capital while keeping costs lower.[38]

Following suit, Russia has been seeking to develop an underwater reconnaissance drone, which it hopes to be in service by 2017. The system would be able to remain operational for up to 90 days, giving it the ability to do persistent surveillance for long periods of time while not expending the human capital that would otherwise be required. According to the Russian news service RT, the drone is meant to submerge to 984 ft. in order to keep track of the submarines that the drone is supposed to observe. The drone is also supposed to be operable in the Arctic, which requires a certain degree of hardiness because of the weather and ice in that region.[39]

Both China and India are developing USVs mostly for surveillance. As US Navy Captain Carl Schuster suggested, "the innovations promise to add new strategic dimensions to global maritime hot spots, including simmering tensions in the South China Sea."[40] The United States has been developing a number of unmanned units that it would intend to use for demining, antisubmarine warfare, and antipiracy, so it is not surprising that China would be developing its own systems. China has two known USVs, the first a vessel used for meteorological survey that was also used to support the sailing race in the 2008 Olympics in Beijing, and another a prototype that can be controlled remotely or autonomously, mostly for surveillance.

India's interest in USVs is primarily for antipiracy, in particular being able to deploy an unmanned vehicle to conduct reconnaissance areas in potentially hostile waters. The hope is to develop unmanned ships that can loiter in "the exact area where pirates wait for an assault. This would add power to the first strike capability."[41] The Indian Navy seeks to build on what they view as the success of US and Israeli navies when it comes to unmanned vehicles.[42]

In short, many of the same players in the development of aerial and ground unmanned vehicles are also interested in and developing maritime systems. Whereas the aerial drones have an international regime dedicated to stemming their proliferation, albeit one with limitations, unmanned systems in the maritime environment would face no such proliferation impediments, meaning that those countries seeking to acquire the technology likely can. Whether there are hazards to such proliferation, however, is another question.

Q. Are unmanned maritime systems likely to be game changers?

As the analysis of proliferation suggests, as long as unmanned technologies can circumvent the limitations and risks faced by humans, they will be attractive to states. This includes aerial systems but also underwater or surface systems. Some of the security consequences are therefore analogous across the different types of drones. To the extent that using drones reduces the costs of incursion, states will be tempted and even emboldened to use force across boundaries. Reports of Russian submarines entering Sweden's waters have already emerged, including a newly released report in 2015.[43] To the extent that the costs of these incursions drop when the technology is unmanned, we might expect more such incursions. If the rules of engagement are unclear when the vehicle is manned, they are even murkier with unmanned systems. Can countries send USVs across boundaries without paying any consequences or will the other side consider this an incursion that requires a response? These questions have gone unanswered but the indeterminate rules of engagement raise the prospect of miscalculation.

Aerial drones launched from aircraft carriers have the potential to be game changers in ways similar to those launched from land. In some ways, however, that effect would be influenced by the enormous array of ships. To be sure, they cannot reach far-flung destinations as quickly as aircraft, but they could essentially provide a forward operating base from which combat operations could be launched, for example with the UCLASS. If other countries came to possess similar technologies, they too could deploy combat drones from a ship. One scenario could include Russia or China deploying a naval ship to the Western Hemisphere and putting a new type of aircraft in range of the United States, which could seem attractive to states that do not have forward operating bases in the hemisphere.

One of the most significant game changers is the development of autonomy in naval drone technology. In this context, autonomy would relate to the ability to set a destination and for the underwater drone to reach the destination without human operation, which can mean guiding its course based on attributes along the sea floor, through bridges, or other features of the underwater environment. Autonomy is important for maritime environments since they can free underwater vehicles from the umbilical cable. Otherwise, this cable is required for power and data from the mother vessel, which then needs to be in the vicinity. Autonomous unmanned alternatives allow for a greater range and maneuverability.

In terms of positive developments, unmanned technologies offer a world of lower-risk options for a range of activities, from antipiracy to exploration of areas that would otherwise be off limits because of ice or cold, such as Antarctica. For now, however, the technology continues to evolve, which is made more difficult by ongoing debates about requirements and budgetary constraints, and also technological impediments presented by the difficulty of navigating the complex maritime environment, including everything from boat traffic, to unpredictable currents, to debris on the ocean floor.

Q. Are there nonmilitary applications of unmanned maritime technologies?

As with the use of aerial drones, unmanned maritime technologies have also been gaining traction for nonmilitary purposes. As *National Defense* magazine observed in 2012, part of the reason for the "market cross" of underwater drones, in which primarily defense companies such as Boeing and Lockheed begin trying to sell technology in commercial markets, is that defense budgets had been in decline.[44] Moreover, for some of the most fruitful applications, such as oil and gas, early exploration had uncovered the low-hanging fruit and the next frontier consisted of either remote areas such as the poles or deep water, neither of which makes for easy work for manned alternatives.

Indeed, the most lucrative application of unmanned maritime systems is certainly in the service of the oil and gas industry, where these unmanned vehicles have been used for deep-sea surveys that allow companies to make maps before investing in infrastructure. These unmanned systems became prevalent in the early 1980s as a way to explore deep-sea oil fields that were beyond the reach of human divers, then plateaued in their development as the price of oil came down in the mid-1980s, and again accelerated so that these vehicles can be used for identification of the fields, sea development, and repair and maintenance.

Unmanned underwater vehicles are also touted for their ability to promote research in areas of the ocean that are too remote or dangerous for humans, for example, as a way to discover the underside of the Arctic and Antarctica. While altogether too cold and unwieldy for humans, these drones could be able to probe the underside of the sea ice, mapping features such as algae that allow scientists to understand the food chain in ways that they were unable to do when only marine creatures or specially trained divers were able to access the underwater algae. The diving drones, shaped like torpedoes, are launched from holes in the ice. Scientists drill these holes using oil burners and steam drills and then deploy the torpedo-like drones. Those drones then collect measurements that allow scientists to extrapolate the overall amount of algae under the ice.[45]

Similarly, unmanned underwater vehicles took over aspects of the search for Malaysian Airlines Flight 370, which proved vexing in part because of the enormous area that the search spanned. The Bluefin-21 was able to produce high resolution, 3D mapping of the sea floor and go to an area that an Australian Air Chief Marshal designated as "new to man."[46] While it was an unmanned submarine that conducted this particular search, unmanned surface vehicles could carry out analogous functions.

Beyond these applications, there are also recreational uses of UUVs. Given the sophistication required to operate in the open seas, and the comparatively limited expertise of hobbyists, these unmanned vehicles tend not to go too far afield; nevertheless, this wider interest in UUVs is demonstrated by groups such as the Personal Submersibles Organization, whose members use the Internet to compare notes on how best to design, build, and operate personal underwater vehicles, both manned and unmanned, in their capacity as hobbyists.

5

NONCOMBAT TECHNOLOGY

The use of drones for armed conflict has tended to draw a good deal of scrutiny and indeed criticism, but drones have potential uses far beyond combat. This chapter, which returns the focus to aerial drones because of where many of the developments have been, evaluates the role of unmanned aerial technology for nonlethal purposes, from security objectives such as humanitarian crisis prevention, to immigration enforcement, to commercial deliveries. Nonmilitary drone avionics generally fall into one of two categories: rotary drones and fixed-wing drones. Rotary drones are able to hover and move in any direction, making them ideal for capturing pictures and video, spying, and potentially delivering packages. The battery life of these drones is roughly 30 minutes, requiring them to be used within a short range of their operator. Fixed-wing drones can generally fly for far longer than rotary drones, though they are typically more expensive and can require runways for takeoff and landing. On the other hand, this makes them ideal for surveying and maintenance operations. They cannot hover and do not maneuver particularly well.[1] This chapter discusses the emerging non-military applications for these technologies.

Q. Are drones being incorporated into government agencies other than the military?

While the military has been on the leading edge of drone development, government agencies other than the military are increasingly looking to drones to carry out their work. For example, the largest drone fleet outside the Defense Department belongs to Customs and Border Protection. The United States has operated 10 Predator B drones for border control, six on the southwestern border, two on the northern border, and two at Cape Canaveral in Florida. The first use of drones by the agency took place in 2005. Border Patrol agents used them to watch over the US-Mexico border in areas that were inaccessible or dangerous.[2]

The use of these Predators, an unarmed version of those used in conflict, have not been without controversy. The civil liberties group Electronic Frontier Foundation filed a lawsuit that uncovered information showing that Customs and Border Protection flew 700 surveillance missions between 2010 and 2012 for other agencies that were not authorized to use drones for patrol purposes, like the Drug Enforcement Agency.[3]

Questions also arise as to the relative effectiveness of using drones for border control. The drones saw little of the expected airtime that the Customs and Border Protection agency had anticipated. The 10 Predators only logged 5,102 hours in the 2013 fiscal year, a quarter of what the agency had projected. The rate of use fell short of the agency's expectations that drones would be valuable in apprehending individuals illegally crossing the border. In fact, a 2014 audit showed that while costing $12,255 per hour, about five-times the amount anticipated by Customs and Border Protection, drones only aided about 2% of border apprehensions. A spokesperson from the agency defended the use of drones, suggesting that the data was misleading insofar as drones are used for the "big-picture" issues of identifying hot spots rather than tracking individual violators, although the audit concluded by recommending against the agency's proposal of spending an additional $443 million to buy 14 new drones.[4]

As the Customs and Border Protection agency's defense suggests, drones look increasingly appealing for law enforcement, and a number of state and local agencies share the sentiment. Drones can serve similar functions as police helicopters but at a fraction of the cost: $22,000 for a drone compared to between $500,000 and $3 million for a helicopter.[5] The police force in Grand Forks, ND is one of about a dozen in the United States known to use drones. They were also the first police department in the United States to be granted federal approval to fly drones at night. As of late 2015, the police force had flown drones on 11 active missions since beginning to test them. One of these missions involved using thermal imaging to search a large field for two suspects. Another mission involved taking footage outside an apartment window in order to show that a man accused of stalking and raping two college students had a clear view from his apartment to theirs. Five missions involved taking aerial photos of the scene of a crime or traffic accident; in two missions a drone was used to assess the flooding of a river; in the other two missions a drone aided in separate searches for missing people.[6]

Other police departments are attempting to integrate drones into their policing strategies as well. In April 2014, the city of Lloydminster became the first city in Canada to use drones for speed and traffic law enforcement, with the city citing lower costs than existing approaches. That said, the city also recognized the potential anxiety that drones might create among a public that would not have the same predictability of knowing where photo enforcement units sit.[7]

Indeed, even the *potential* use of drones for law enforcement has unnerved the public. Even before being taken out of the box, the Los Angeles Police Department's plans to use two drones—obtained by the Seattle Police Department—for law enforcement met with enormous public backlash, driven by concerns about privacy. One organization, called the "Stop LAPD Spying Coalition," has tried to mobilize opposition to the use of drones for law enforcement, cautioning about police militarization and spying.[8] In response, the LAPD has sought to assuage concerns, with the LAPD Inspector General promising a moratorium on drones for law enforcement and reporting that the drones were transferred to his custody where they would be secured, not released or used in any manner.

If the Seattle Police Department's experience with drones is any guide, the political headwinds against the LAPD using drones for law enforcement may prove too strong. Several years back, the Seattle Police Department had received a Department of Homeland Security grant to investigate traffic incidents, homicides, and hazardous materials with two drones. Ultimately, following vociferous public opposition, the Seattle mayor had to "pull the plug on a plan to let the Seattle Police Department begin use of two drones it purchased through a federal grant."[9] Instead, the police department bequeathed its drones to the LAPD at no cost to the LAPD. The Seattle Police Department declared that it had worked with state and federal agencies to find a new home for the department's drones, transferring them to the Los Angeles Police Department, while not being under any obligation to repay the federal grant that had sponsored the original drone acquisition. Of course the LAPD proceeded to encounter the same hostility that their colleagues up the coast had received.

Q. What are the potential commercial applications of drones?

Amazon made news in 2014 by announcing that it would deliver packages via drone, and in some doing joined what has become a growing tide of commercial drone interest. The Association for Unmanned Vehicle Systems International (AUVSI), a drone trade group, estimates that the commercial drone industry would be worth $13.6 billion within three years of current legislative restrictions on commercial drone use being lifted and $82 billion between 2015 and 2025. They also predict that this growth in industry would create 100,000 jobs.[10] An engineer from British Aerospace's Autonomous Systems Technology Related Airborne Evaluation and Assessment Team projected a global market of $62 billion per year by 2020 and an overall market worth more than $400 billion based on what they see as a potential windfall coming from maturing technologies and increasing permissiveness at the domestic level.[11]

The list of commercial applications for drones is extensive and includes almost any activity for which surveillance, monitoring, and data are useful and for which there are, as mentioned before, impediments to humans conducting a task that is "dull, dirty, or dangerous." In response to the increased demand for commercial drones, the Federal Aviation Administration (FAA) has been granting exemptions at increasingly fast rates to drones that "do not pose a threat to national airspace users or national security."[12]

One of the earliest applications of drones for commercial activities has been in the area of oil and gas. Launched by hand into the air, drones use sensors to generate 3D images and "paint" maps of the ground. Drones are useful in this context in part because of the remoteness of the Prudhoe Bay, which is in the Northern Slope of Alaska and home to the largest oil fields in the United States. Similarly, the climate of the region means that many of the roads are unpassable many months, giving a great advantage to aerial drones. As Secretary of Transportation Anthony Foxx endorsed the move to use drones "these surveys on Alaska's North Slope are another important step toward broader commercial use of unmanned aircraft. The technology is quickly changing, and the opportunities are growing."[13]

A second early mover in terms of commercial drones has been in the construction industry. As *Architect* magazine puts it, "interest in drones is on the rise among architecture and construction firms for the equipment's ability to access and scope out hard-to-reach or dangerous sites."[14] This industry is particularly interested in aerial imagery that can be used for surveying and logistical planning. Drones also help monitor progress and enable engineers to work in real-time on the implementation of a construction project. As the CEO of a drone start-up Skycatch speculates, "one job site could cost a company a few billion dollars. If you can shave a few days off their costs, it's huge."[15] In a round of FAA approvals announced in December 2014, Clayco Corp., a company able to monitor construction sites, was granted an exemption. The FAA is still requiring that they fly under 400 ft., fly within sight of operators, and be under 55 lb. The technology will "help with topographic surveys, environmental site assessment, [and] job site safety."[16]

A third emerging area for commercial drones is in agriculture. The AUVSI "found that almost all respondents considered agriculture to be far and above the largest market."[17] According to *Aviation Week*, about 80% of future commercial applications of drones would likely involve agriculture.[18] One scholar working on agricultural drones suggested that "the application of these data drones is only limited by our imagination."[19] For less than $1,000 farmers could have a drone, typically a Quadcopter or equivalent, that allows farmers to fly autonomously using a global positioning system (GPS) and take images that are then incorporated into software. As Chris Anderson, formerly of *Wired* magazine describes it, the imagery can be used in the service of visualizing patterns of soil variation and pest infestations; observing differences between crops that are healthy and those that are not through the infrared data captured; and creating time-series animations. These tools allow any warning signs to pop up early so that farmers can address emerging problems with their crops, using the drone to assess crops, monitor the health of crops, and ensure resistance to pests, all of which are currently tasks that require a farmer to walk through the fields.

Agriculture's turn to drones meshes with what has become the trend of "increasingly data-driven" or "precision" agriculture aimed at becoming more efficient to help growing populations. This approach is based on observations of variation within and across crops through the use of imagery. The introduction of GPS made it possible to map terrain and then observe spatial variation on the basis of crop yield, hydration, and nutrient levels in ways that optimize decisions about where to plant, how to combat disease, and where to irrigate. While this approach has leveraged satellite technology, the rotation of satellites makes them better suited to observing bigger-picture problems over a longer period of time. One robotics engineer suggested, "it sounds trivial but those numbers really add up a lot. If we could save farms 1% on inputs like herbicide and pesticide and increase their yields by 1%, you are looking at multibillion dollar savings."[20]

Internet giants have also been keen to get in on the action. Facebook and Google have both pursued drones to help provide more widespread Internet access. Facebook has shown interest in buying solar-powered drones, which can stay airborne for up to five years and could act as wireless access points to provide Internet in remote areas. In pursuing this interest, Facebook bought Ascenta, a UK-based company that makes solar-powered drones. Google also acquired a solar-powered drone company that Facebook had been trying to acquire, namely, Titan Aerospace, and then more recently created a new parent company, called Alphabet, which would recognize that the company is much more than a search engine, but rather a holding company for everything, including its drone delivery business. Google has conducted experiments in Australia that would use fixed-wing aircraft to deliver anything from chocolate to cattle vaccines. Following in Google's footsteps, Amazon announced that it would offer PrimeAir in the near future, which would deliver packages via drone. The company has requested permission from the FAA to test drones capable of flying for 30 minutes to deliver packages up 7 lb., a weight which covers 86% of Amazon's products. The letter to the FAA argues that "granting this request will do nothing more than allow Amazon to do what thousands of hobbyists and manufacturers of model aircraft do every day, and we will abide by much stronger safety measures than currently required for these groups by FAA policies and regulations."[21]

The use of drones for deliveries is attractive because it means accessing areas that are currently too expensive to reach, too dangerous, or inaccessible via conventional delivery services. It is for this reason that DHL, the German logistics company, launched a service to use an autonomous Quadcopter to deliver supplies to Germany's North Sea island of Juist, which is also car-free. According to *Deutsche Post*, which owns DHL, it had authorization from the German transport ministry to fly only its parcelcopter only to Juist and not to fly over houses. DHL reports that it avoids air collisions by flying under about 167 ft. (50 m) while checking in with a ground station. It also uses a container that is weatherproof to protect packages from potential damage.[22] UPS and FedEx appear to be following suit in trying to develop drones for delivery services. All of these will require permission from the FAA, and will most likely need permission to use drones outside the line of sight of the operator.

The pioneer for this model of delivery drones was a Silicon Valley startup called Matternet. They assert that "drone delivery should be first used in the developing world to deliver food, medicine, and other necessities to areas that are less accessible by car or truck."[23] The company has argued that commercial technology usually diffuses from developed to developing countries, even though those who need the technology most are arguably people in developing countries who otherwise cannot access medicine or food because they live in remote areas with poor infrastructure. The idea behind Matternet is to build a network of drones that can cover a swath of land by transporting goods between ground stations, which will recharge batteries and load swap in ways that sidestep roads altogether. The group has tested the network of octocopters in the Dominican Republic, Haiti, and Lesotho, where it transported material from clinics to hospital labs, with visions for trying a broader-scale implementation in the coming years. As the *IEEE Spectrum* suggested, "Amazon's talk of package delivery drones may just be pie-in-the-sky, but start-up Matternet has already begun testing a delivery-drone network in developing countries."[24]

Drones also seem to have promise for the film and journalism industries because many potential scenes or stories would fit under the "dangerous" heading of "dull, dirty, or dangerous" when it comes to human involvement. For Hollywood, several companies have used drones on closed sets not only as a cost-effective alternative for aerial shots normally performed by helicopters or planes but as one that can capture something like an explosive action scene that might put a cameraman in danger.[25] The cable news network CNN also reported that it had brokered a deal with the FAA to incorporate drones into its reporting. "Our aim is to get beyond hobby-grade equipment and establish what options are available and workable to produce high-quality video journalism using various types of UAVs (drones) and camera setups," according to one senior vice president, who followed by saying that the drones would naturally have to operate safely. CNN and the FAA have also partnered with Georgia Tech to study how drones might best be used in the service of journalism.[26] For now, the collaborators are simply testing for ways that would "advance efforts to integrate Unmanned Aerial Vehicles (UAVs) into newsgathering and reporting."[27]

The sports network ESPN has also begun using drones to cover sporting events such as the Winter X Games, with the provision that ESPN would keep drones within a "closed-set environment." This has been defined as not over spectators or near the airport but rather to track snowboardcross or snowmobiling activities. ESPN uses drones for closer coverage of the events. ESPN's manager for the approval process stated that "any piece of technology we feel brings viewers closer to the event, we're interested in."[28] Russia also approved the use of drones to capture snowboard and skiing events at the Sochi Olympics, which allowed for some viewing angles that would be impossible with either a distant helicopter or an individual photographer from a more distant vantage point.

Q. What are the potential applications of drones for aid and relief operations?

Although much of the publicity about drones often highlights the negative security and privacy, drones also have the potential to have salutary impacts. For example, wildlife researchers have been using drones carrying cameras and sensors to track and document wildlife, estimate population sizes, map terrain, and catch poachers in areas of Africa, South Asia, and more recently Latin America.[29] For example, Mexico has planned to use drones to detect illegal fishing of porpoises in the Sea of Cortez. As a government official observed, "drones would allow us to have permanent aerial patrols in the area and be able to react much more efficiently and quickly" to protect the porpoises, which are fewer than 100 in number and threatened by the same nets that fish for the totoaba, a fish that is highly sought after by chefs in China.[30]

A number of actors have sought to promote the idea further. Princess Aliyah Pandolfi of Kashmir-Robotics founded the Wildlife Conservation UAV (Drone) Challenge. The challenge, to design inexpensive drones capable of detecting and locating poachers, attracted close to 140 entries. The drones must also be able to be launched from the bush, operate for hours at a time, and communicate over existing commercial infrastructures.[31] Google gave the World Wildlife Fund $5 million for anti-poaching drones, which have conducted aerial surveillance in isolated areas of Africa and Asia, where poaching of endangered species is common.[32] These drones are often launched by hand and are equipped with night vision capabilities to see poachers in all levels of light. The visual information coming from the drones is then communicated to rangers, who can apprehend the poachers. More generally, drones could be useful for documenting wildlife that is difficult to reach otherwise, such as killer whales and osprey. They are able to conduct flyovers and document population size without disturbing the animals to the extent that a fixed-wing, manned aircraft would. Recognition technology that could differentiate between different species is also being developed.

Another application of drones with considerable upsides is the use of drones for disaster relief. Drones have the virtue of being able to access areas of an earthquake relief zone, for example, that would be inaccessible to humans. For example, in the wake of the 7.8-magnitude Nepal earthquake in 2015, relief workers were struggling to reach some of the areas that had been impacted most severely. Aid organizations began turning to drones to reach these areas in ways that individuals could not. For example, the aid organization GlobalMedic used three drones to locate trapped individuals via thermal cameras mounted onto drones. The drones could also use aerial mapping to create a picture of the areas in highest need and then focus food assistance to those areas. In an area with a shortage of resources and poor infrastructure, being able to triage based on this drone footage was extremely helpful.

Drones for these purposes followed the example of the 2011 Japan Fukushima nuclear accident, in which drones were used to identify radiation levels so that individuals did not have to be exposed to potentially dangerous radiation levels themselves. A Japanese company has subsequently developed a drone that can fly into the Fukushima reactor autonomously, using lasers to avoid obstacles and recharging batteries without human intervention. One robotics company, Autonomous Control Systems Laboratory Ltd, created a 1-meter-wide, six-propeller drone to collect dust for examination and measure radiation levels, producing data in real-time.

Another emerging application suitable to aid and relief missions that are often too dangerous for manned equivalents is the use of drones to fight wildfires. In 2015, the National Park Service used surveillance drones such as the catapult-launched ScanEagle to provide information about the fire in Olympic National Park. The area was remote, with much of the terrain inaccessible, and the drone was able to map the most intense hot spots, while also guiding water drops in a more efficient way. The California National Guard had similarly used drones in 2013 to do infrared mapping of the Yosemite National Park fire, and drones have also been used for remote fires in Alaska. The FAA had to provide temporary waivers and certificates in each case, but the appealing aspect of using drones for these cases was to spare pilots their lives in what is often a hazardous duty. Drones have also drawn ire in the context of wildfires, however; not the officially sanctioned ones but the hobbyist aircraft that have interfered with wildfire management and caused firefighters to ground the planes they were using to fight the fires. The Board of Supervisors in San Bernardino, California, offered a $75,000 reward for information about several incidents of drone interference, and the FAA has indicated that it will crack down on recreational drone users who create public safety hazards.

The use of drones for aid and relief has no doubt produced efficient relief provision but some of the bad apples cited above has created something of an uphill battle for doing so. The American Red Cross has conducted a study to investigate how it might be able to use drones for disaster response and relief, and while it has identified many potential opportunities, it also raised some questions about regulations and the policy environment in which the drones would operate. For example, groups wanting to use drones for the 2014 Washington State mudslide relief effort were rebuffed by government officials concerned about how the drones might be used. A United Nations humanitarian affairs official who conducted a study on the use of drones for humanitarian responses concluded that the pendulum may have swung too far in the direction of restrictiveness: "It's been interesting to see how fast we went from total Wild West to something where it's rapidly shifting to the default is that you can't do it without permission, but there's not necessarily clear rules for how do you get permission."[33]

Q. What are the potential applications for recreational drones?

Like commercial drones, recreational drones are a growing industry, with drone manufacturers reporting revenue growth of three to five *hundred* percent per year. In 2014, the fourth-most-searched item under "I want to buy" is "drone."[34]

Chris Anderson's assessment of the individual interest in drones revealed about 1,000 new personal drones enter the skies every month.[35] The Do-It-Yourself Drones community, a community composed of individuals who assemble their own drones or assemble those of premade kits they buy online, had 26,000 members as of 2012. Their membership tripled to 61,000 by 2014.[36] As one technology outlet observed: "if the recent holiday season (2014) seemed like a big one for drones, brace yourself, because it's just the beginning. The global market for drones will climb to at least $1 billion by 2018." This would represent an enormous increase from the Consumer Electronics Association's forecast of $130 million for 2015.[37]

These personal technologies include inexpensive toy drones marketed toward young teenagers. More advanced drones are also available for individual use for photography and videography. The most popular hobby drone has been the Chinese-made DJI's Phantom 2 Vision+, a roughly $1,000 drone with a mounted camera device and a GPS for stabilizing the drone in windy conditions.[38]

Drones are appealing to individuals and hobbyists interested not just in new technologies in their own right but also in the instant and intimate documentation of their experiences. As Anderson suggests:

> If you're a windsurfer and want a great Youtube video of your exploits, you're not going to get that from the shore, and hiring a manned helicopter and camera crew to follow you offshore isn't cheap. But if you've got a "Followme" box on your belt, you can just press a button and a quadcopter drone with a camera can take off from the shore, position itself 30 feet up and 30 feet away from you and automatically follow you as you skim the waves, camera trained on you the whole way.[39]

That technology then becomes smaller and lighter and can be placed on a soccer ball to follow youth sport, or can bring new meaning to "helicopter parenting" by tracking a son or daughter on his or her way to a bus stop or school. Knowing that the FAA's 400-ft. operating regulation is difficult to enforce, some companies are considering incorporating altitude and geographic restrictions to help self-regulate the industry. This is intended to allay any concern about potential collisions that could set back the rapid growth that the civilian drone industry is seeing. In other words, a drone manufacturer's device getting sucked into a commercial jet and causing safety concerns for hundreds of passengers may not be good public relations for that company. Nor will it help business since such incidents are likely to trigger a backlash and more restrictive regulations. Several companies are hoping to preempt such regulation by programming in these restrictions while also educating the users of the technology so that they exercise more restraint and caution.[40]

Q. What are the potential safety risks of nonmilitary drone use?

The potential safety risks of unregulated drone use are nontrivial. A number of dangerous incidents involving drones have been reported as individuals have increasingly invested in drones. According to former New York Police Department (NYPD) Commissioner Ray Kelly, the NYPD is still coming to terms with how to think about the use of individual drones because the technology has led the policy to date.[41] Indeed, a number of incidents in the New York metropolitan area highlight the potential for concern when it comes to unfettered drone use in densely populated pedestrian areas and airspace. Hardly a month passes where there is not some news report about a commercial airline having to maneuver to avoid colliding with drones in the New York area.

In one of the early publicized episodes on May 29, 2014, three commercial airliners reported seeing small drones at high altitudes. One plane was descending toward LaGuardia and saw a drone at an altitude of about 5,500 ft. above Manhattan. In July 2014, two Manhattan residents were arrested and charged with first-degree reckless endangerment after two drones they were controlling nearly collided with an NYPD helicopter.[42] Similarly, in November 2014, recreational drones nearly collided with a commercial airliner near John F. Kennedy Airport and earlier in that same week an NYPD helicopter reported a drone flying at 500 ft. and within 4 miles of La Guardia Airport. The latter incident violated the FAA requirement that pilots notify the airport or air traffic control when flying within 5 miles of an airport; the drone also violated the FAA's drone altitude restrictions.[43] The list of such incidents is extensive and growing. In 2014, the FAA reported that it was receiving about 25 notifications of drone sightings or near-encounters per month, including fixed-wing and helicopter drones, amounting to a total of 23 accidents and 236 unsafe incidents stemming from civilian drone use. Theses events are likely to become more common as personal use of drones becomes more popular.

The concerns about individual drone proliferation are not limited to the United States. During October and November 2014, there were a number of sightings of small drones flying over French nuclear reactors. It is still not clear why the drones were flying over the reactors, although one hypothesis is that that they were an "organized provocation" from an antinuclear group. Because the drones are so small and seem to have little more than photo/video capabilities, many do not see them as an immediate threat to the reactors. French officials are, however, taking the matter seriously. Michael Sordi, a lawmaker from Haut-Rhin, warns, "It may be time to start shooting them down, to move to another level of security and sanctions against this behavior." French law forbids flying an aircraft below 3,280 ft. and within 3.1 miles of a nuclear plant. This violation is punishable by one year in prison and a fine of 75,000 euros. In France there are roughly 900 commercial operators and an unknown number of private operators of drones.[44]

The prospect of nonmilitary drones creating safety concerns took on additional relevance in February 2015, when drones were seen flying over Paris at night, near the Eiffel Tower, Louvre, and the US Embassy. While they were initially dismissed as a prank, the Paris police later held three Al-Jazeera journalists on suspicion of flying drones without a license in France, which is illegal and carries a one-year (maximum) sentence. In the wake of the 2015 killings of *Charlie Hebdo* journalists, where society was concerned about follow-up attacks, the unattributed drones flying in Paris created substantial unease.

With this type of unauthorized flying of nonmilitary drones in mind, reports indicate that British nuclear plants represent a visible landmark. The United Kingdom has 16 operational reactors that produce about 18% of the country's electricity. John Large, a British nuclear expert, assessed the vulnerability in saying that "the flexible access of maneuverability of the drones" is such that they can transgress barriers that ground vehicles or even manned aircraft might have a difficult time transgressing.[45] To be sure, small drones would have trouble penetrating cement walls, but one view is that the drones could be used in reconnaissance to identify structural weaknesses that are then used to inform aerial attacks that then produce meltdown with widespread effects. A campaign event for German Chancellor Angela Merkel in September 2013 was interrupted as a small drone flew toward the podium. The drone landed on the platform in front of Merkel as the operator was arrested. The German Pirate Party claimed responsibility for this act, wanting to show Merkel what it is like to be observed by a drone. Though this incident seemed to be fairly innocuous, it exposed the possible security concerns associated with drones that can transcend barriers intended for road or foot traffic. Even small drones are easily equipped with weapons that could prove very dangerous if used at a public event.

China is reportedly developing countermeasures for these small drones, with a laser weapon system designed to shoot down drones flying at low altitudes. Chinese officials were particularly worried about security risks associated with small drones, as they are cheap and easy to use, making them ideal for terrorists. Similarly, the US military has been moving forward on laser-based systems that can eliminate drones by literally burning them from the sky. Although development remains at the proof-of-concept stage, it does point to the potential of the technology in the future, though as one laser scientist pointed out, "the path to laser weapons is littered with dead lasers."[46]

Q. What are the potential privacy risks associated with domestic drones?

Drones could make many tasks such as delivering packages, conducting law enforcement, and surveying property cheaper and easier. The increasing prevalence has drawn ire from privacy advocates, however, who worry about the ways that drones seem to present new and pernicious infringement of individual space. What makes surveillance technologies potentially different is that drones, especially miniaturized ones, can hide in plain sight. One website advertises the Dragonfly drone as "a palm-sized robot that flies like a bird and hovers like an insect." Because of the size, which is small, and the appearance, which mimics a dragonfly, one website brags that when it comes to insects and drones, "People can't tell the difference!"[47] The ability to fly without being noticed means that these drones can be more intrusive than other surveillance technologies without fear of being spotted.

Even for larger-scale drones used for personal or government purposes, which people can identify in ways that draw attention to the possible surveillance and photography function, some groups see drones as presenting a new and serious privacy threat. The difference with other forms of surveillance is that they are relatively inexpensive, can loiter for long periods, and can penetrate into areas that might have been off limits to surveillance cameras mounted on street lights. With the proliferation of drones for domestic use in mind, two related potential problems arise in terms of privacy. One deals with the government's use of drones in a US homeland setting and the other addresses privacy infractions resulting from the use of private or commercial drones. This section addresses the privacy concerns related to both government and private drones and then investigates the extent to which current constitutional protections will be sufficient to address the drone-related privacy concerns.

In terms of privacy issues related to the government use of drones, with even the current technology, drones could be barely discernible in the sky but still allow the government to collect video or images with impressive resolution. Senator Rand Paul raised the rhetorical question in an op-ed of whether "unwarranted and constant surveillance by an aerial eye of Big Government" was the answer to crime. Senator Paul went on to state that he did not want a government drone monitoring his barbecues or "a nanny state watching over my every move."[48] He then wrote a series of letters to Robert Mueller, Director of the Federal Bureau of Investigation. The first requested more information about how long the FBI had been using drones while not publicly outlining protection of privacy, whether it had planned to develop such protections, the measures it was taking to protect Fourth Amendment rights, along with a litany of other concerns related to the FBI's use of drones, including whether it planned to arm them.[49] Another followed up on the earlier email, reiterating the importance of transparency and requesting that the FBI offer prompt responses to the queries. He then sent an additional letter asking for clarification on the FBI's response that there had not been a need to seek a warrant to use drones in the past, seeking to understand the FBI's understanding of when individuals do or do not have reasonable expectations of privacy, the matter on which the Fourth Amendment turns.

The American Civil Liberties Union reported approvingly on Senator Paul's "dogged" efforts to gain clarity on what it means to have a "reasonable expectation of privacy."[50] The

Federal Bureau of Investigation responded to these requests stating that its agents had used drones to conduct surveillance over the United States 10 times between 2006 and 2013, using the drones to support operations related to kidnappings, search and rescue missions, drug interdictions, and support missions. It noted that it had conducted surveillance using drones for eight criminal and two national security cases. The FBI elaborated that it does not use armed drones over US soil and that it would acquire a warrant to obtain information that goes beyond a reasonable expectation of privacy. Otherwise though, the FBI concluded that there were no Fourth Amendment concerns surrounding its use of drones.[51] In a follow-up letter to members of Congress, the legislative affairs officer for the FBI noted that it was unable to disclose many of the FBI-specific drone practices, which are classified as "Law Enforcement Sensitive" because of the security considerations with which they deal.[52]

Given the fraught nature of the discussion about privacy, including surrounding the term "reasonable," it is not surprising that the United States has had a number of Supreme Court cases interpreting the scope of what is reasonable or not. In three major Supreme Court cases in the 1980s, the justices sided with the government. These cases very much foreshadowed the present debate surrounding the use of drones by law enforcement agencies. The first case in 1986, *California v. Ciraolo*, dealt with whether the government could constitutionally identify marijuana plants in an individual's backyard from an airplane at 1,000 ft. The court stated that the "Fourth Amendment simply does not require the police traveling in the public airways at this altitude to obtain a warrant in order to observe what is visible to the naked eye." In another case, *Dow Chemical Co. v. United States*, the use of government cameras to take aerial pictures of a Dow chemical facility was seen as constitutional in part because "the photographs here are not so revealing of intimate details as to raise constitutional concerns," as the Court put it. In other words, these rulings suggested that the mere involvement of technology did not itself constitute a violation of privacy under the Constitution since these technologies were not being used in superhuman ways but rather completely consistent with the human eye and to view events not of an intimate nature. Thus, in some respects one could be wary of the proliferation of drones from a privacy perspective.

Despite these concerns, others suggest that the proliferation of drones presents few risks even when it comes to questions of privacy. One argument suggests that the privacy horse has left the barn long before drones came onto the scene. As the Congressional Research Service's report on privacy and drones puts it, "in determining society's privacy expectations, a reviewing court might also take into consideration the proliferation of aerial mapping such as Google Maps and Google Earth conducted by private actors."[53] For that matter, do the technologies depart considerably from a closed-circuit surveillance camera strapped onto a lamppost instead of a drone? Are individuals simply responding differently because of the novelty of the technology but not because of any qualitative difference between the privacy they have already relinquished and that which they would stand to relinquish with drones? Drones, according to this logic, are if anything a difference of degree, not a difference of kind.

Another defense of drones expresses full confidence in the Constitution's ability to protect individuals' privacy. Albeit speaking from the perspective of having a dog in the fight, the AUVSI has expressed agreement with this position, suggesting that existing constitutional provisions protect privacy: "Over the last 225 years, the court system has done a pretty good job of protecting our Fourth Amendment rights, and that is something we absolutely support."[54] Indeed, many types of drones would fall outside the "naked-eye" provision and be unconstitutional, and several cases point to important privacy protections under the Fourth Amendment. In one case, *Kyllo v. United States*, the Supreme Court decided the constitutionality of a government thermal imager to identify illegal marijuana growing and raised concerns about whether permitting the government to collect information through "advancing technology" was reasonable. The technology went beyond the "human eye" in using an imaging system that was found, in turn, to reach beyond the limits of constitutionality. As John Villasenor from UCLA Law School concludes, "under a balanced reading of *Kyllo*, the government use of a UAV to reveal 'details of the home that would previously have been unknowable without physical intrusion' would be unconstitutional today."[55]

More contemporary cases involve the legality of GPS tracking devices that the government affixed to a vehicle without obtaining warrants. These cases were both considered of questionable constitutionality, with Supreme Court justices across the ideological spectrum expressing the view that new technologies such as GPS monitoring went beyond "reasonable societal expectation of privacy," as Justice Sotomayor put it, a view shared by Justices Scalia and Alito. These cases point to the prospect not of drones running rampant in the infringement of privacy but of reaching some constitutional bounds in the form of the Fourth Amendment.[56]

The rapidly changing technology, increasing use of drones by law enforcement and private citizens, ambiguity surrounding the parameters of an individual's right against "unreasonable searches and seizures," and the definition of what constitutes a "search" point toward the likelihood that a number of drone-specific legal cases will soon fill courts around the country. Andrew Couts, writing for *Digital Trends*, observes that these questions are "slippery" under the best circumstances: "throw drones in the mix and . . . the fine line across which surveillance by the state becomes 'search' gets downright knotty."[57]

The privacy issues surrounding individuals' use of drones raise a somewhat different set of considerations. Those involving the government use of drones more directly hinge on questions of constitutionality, primarily through the Fourth Amendment protections, and generally raise more serious opposition, in part because government drones are generally more capacious, and individuals may fear some inappropriate government use of the information obtained through a drone. For the use of individual drones, the concern is more simply about the invasion of one's own privacy. Individuals worry, for example, about whether previously intimate activities such as sunbathing at a nude beach would become matters of public consumption. Indeed, there are a number of videos online showing footage from a drone loitering over such a beach. As a Brookings Institution report on privacy concludes, "there is no firm consensus about how best to safeguard privacy rights from nongovernmental drone surveillance."[58] These privacy matters reside at the state level, which has given rise to considerable interstate variation depending on philosophies about the balance between the individual's right to engage in drone hobbyist activity and an individual's right to privacy. Whereas some states have passed "peeping Tom" laws in the context of drones, others have remained mum.

Q. Does the public support the use of domestic drones?

In terms of the American public, which has generated the most extensive opinion data, Americans are generally supportive of using armed drones for counterterrorism abroad, but are more ambivalent when it comes to the use of drones for law enforcement and domestic surveillance. While 44% of Americans approve of using drones to assist with police work, 36% disapprove, and 17% are neutral. Of those queried about domestic drones 35% indicated that they were extremely or very concerned about the potential loss of privacy from police surveillance compared to 36% that were not concerned (another 24% indicated that they were somewhat concerned). The CEO of the National Constitution Center, David Eisner, indicated that he "had assumed that the idea that American police would be using the same technology that our military is using in

Afghanistan would garner an almost hysterical response." He attributed this attitude to the populace's sense of insecurity and willingness to trade off civil liberties in exchange for more security.[59]

A year later, in a different poll, 65% of Americans reported opposition to the use of unmanned drones by police agencies in the United States.[60] Similar concerns were raised several months later when 58% of Americans expressed that police departments were "going too far" in their use of "drones, military weapons and armored vehicles," with only 37% indicating that these technologies were necessary.[61]

A more detailed set of polls helped unpack the aspects of drones by law enforcement that individuals find objectionable. Table 5.1 summarizes poll responses for a range of activities involving the use of drones. As the table suggests, Americans tend to support drones for security and humanitarian purposes but not for police activities that might have adverse impacts on them, such as issuing speeding tickets. They are also more leery of armed drones than the unarmed drones; for instance, support for armed drones in the service of border control generated far less support than when the drones in question were not specified as armed or unarmed—implying that they were unarmed.

Table 5.1 Public Support for Drones for the Purposes of Law Enforcement, by Activity

Question: "Use of Drones to …"	Support	Oppose	Don't Know
Issue speeding tickets	21%	72%	6%
Control illegal immigration	62%	30%	8%
Help with search and rescue missions	83%	11%	6%
Help hostage situations (armed drones specified)	52%	38%	9%
Patrol border (armed drones specified)	44%	49%	8%

Source: Monmouth University Polling Institute, field dates July 25–30, 2013.

These polls lend some credence to the public's view that domestic drones should be used to bolster security at home while remaining nonintrusive on a day-to-day basis. A separate poll by Duke University and the Institute for Homeland Security Solutions corroborated this intuition. In their poll 67% of the public supported drones for homeland security, 63% for fighting crime, and as high as 88% for search and rescue. Sixty-seven percent of individuals, however, expressed considerable concern about monitoring in public spaces, and 65% are concerned with the potential safety issues of frequent domestic drone use by law enforcement. Support was considerably lower at 26% for the use in traffic violations.[62] The concerns intimated in these studies track fairly closely with the concerns raised by civil liberties groups who worry that drones raise potential privacy issues. The ACLU defends its concerns by citing the Fourth Amendment tenet that people have the right "to be secure in their persons, houses, papers, and effects, against unreasonable searches and seizures." The US government's Congressional Research Service similarly cautioned that "the prospect of drone use inside the United States raises far-reaching issues concerning the extent of government surveillance authority, the value of privacy in the digital age, and the role of Congress in reconciling these issues" in its report on domestic drone use.[63]

Q. How are federal agencies regulating nonmilitary drones?

Currently, the FAA restricts commercial applications of drones as it studies how to incorporate drones safely into national airspace. Until the rules are developed, companies that want to operate drones for commercial purposes must apply to the FAA for an exemption. Those exemptions are increasing quickly. Whereas in April 2015 only about 100 companies had received exemptions, by September that number had reached 700, with as many as 50 exemptions granted per week.

As suggested earlier, some of the drone applications are more controversial than others. For example, those involving agriculture are generally less contentious, in part since they do not generally present the same privacy concerns as flying over a city. Nonetheless, a July 2014 FAA ruling stated that "farmers, ranchers and all commercial operators are prohibited from using UASs until the FAA institutes regulations for the safe integration of UASs into National Airspace."[64] The slight bump in FAA exemptions given to agricultural drones in 2015 suggests that the reins may be loosening slightly. Indeed, Congress tasked the FAA with better integrating commercial drones, rules that seek to balance the safety concerns of having as many as 30,000 drones flying in national airspace by 2030 with industry's concerns that it not forgo the enormous commercial upside of a more permissive policy.[65]

In the meantime, as it drafted these rules, the FAA issued a "myth-busting" public service announcement that sought to clarify a number of misconceptions about its commercial drone policy. Among other things, the FAA first stated that there were already about 7,500 small commercial drones in operation in the United States as of 2014. Second, it offered a reminder that even flying below 400 ft. was not necessarily a legal commercial drone activity. Third, though flying a hobby or recreational drone below 400 ft. is both legal and did not require FAA approval, it must be done following FAA safety guidelines. This regulation precludes flying for remuneration or any type of commercial purpose, which is banned via the FAA Modernization and Reform Act of 2012. The spirit of the regulations, according to Michael Huerta, the Director of the FAA, is to prevent drones from interfering with larger aircraft that carry passengers and whose safety could be compromised if they came into contact with drones.[66] Fourth, flying a commercial drone would continue to require a certificate of waiver or authorization that the FAA would issue on a case-by-case basis and that it had mechanisms at its disposal to ensure compliance with the regulations and exemptions it has issued. Lastly, the FAA conceded that the United States might seem to be lagging behind other countries in terms of commercial drone integration but that the delay is reasonable since the United States has "the busiest, most complex airspace in the world."[67] On the other hand, as later sections will suggest, a better way to state it is that other countries have lagged behind the United States in regulating drones, and are only now catching up policy-wise with the demand in commercial drones.

One of the primary concerns driving FAA regulations of commercial drones is the avoidance of midair collisions. As FAA Director Huerta puts it, the "see-and-avoid" principle is a "bedrock principle of aviation... the pilots take action to avoid one another."[68] With 70,000 flights per day in the United States and commercial and recreational flights operating at various altitudes, "the risk of collision between these users and unmanned aircraft must be adequately mitigated before unmanned aircraft can routinely utilize the national airspace system."[69] A government report concluded that unmanned aircraft did not currently have these capabilities. Strict limits on where drones fly have been imposed, in particular the line-of-sight provision, which helps the drone operator avoid air traffic.[70]

The FAA had also initially stated that they would require private pilot's licenses to maintain a predictive awareness of where other pilots would be operating. Even if drone operators cannot see and avoid other aircraft, at least they would know the rules about what altitudes to use, how high to stay above populated areas, and which direction the oncoming pilot would turn in case of an impending head-on collision. All of these are rules that anyone with a private pilot's license would know. Having initially suggested that certification would entail obtaining a pilot's license, the government appeared to reverse its position on requiring a private pilot's license for obtaining FAA certification to fly commercial drones (those that have received exemptions). Instead, applicants would be required to take an exam that tests basic aeronautical information, emergency procedures, and airspace classification, a much lower barrier to entry for gaining certification than a pilot's license.

While the move away from the pilot's license appeared to be an about-face, the FAA is clearly chasing a moving target. Because of continuous, dramatic changes to the technology, regulations have struggled to keep pace. The FAA is trying to balance what seems like the inexorable push of commercial drone technology, which favors more rapid integration, with the competing pressures of safety, which could push in a more restrictive direction. In response to these challenges, the FAA set up six test locations across the United States. Congress required that the FAA establish six sites that can help test the interaction between drones and manned aircraft, which it has done in Virginia, North Dakota, Alaska, Nevada, Texas, and New York. As the FAA Administrator Michael Huerta advertised, "Having all six national test sites up and running will give us more and better data to help expand the safe use of unmanned aircraft into our airspace."[71]

Drone producers and industries that drones would serve have questioned the regulations discussed above. There are several lines of criticism. One is that the regulations artificially group drones into commercial drones, whose use is currently prohibited, and hobbyists, who fly in their backyard. Commercial drones, this argument goes, are not intrinsically problematic, but become a concern based on where they are used, and hobbyists can actually present problems if they are used in densely populated areas. Rural and urban flight environments are vastly different from each another. For the latter, crowded airspace is a primary concern, but is not an issue for rural flight environments. A farmer using a drone to survey commercial crops is very different than a city-dwelling drone hobbyist taking flight in the city. Context would suggest that the 400-foot ceiling and line-of-sight requirements would be artificial and unnecessary in rural places where drones operate over vast spaces. According to this view, regulations would be based not on commercial versus hobbyist applications but on where the drone flies, whether in crowded urban environments or less densely populated rural ones.

Another criticism deals with the level of training required to operate a drone, with particularly forceful criticism lobbed against the earlier FAA expectation that individuals have a private pilot's license. The FAA had planned to require that drone operators obtain a license, which includes dozens of hours of work with an expensive flight instructor, a medical examination, and many hours of additional classroom time. On the one hand, the proposal seemed sound for the reasons previously mentioned, namely, that individuals operating a drone should also learn where and how to fly in airspace, how to communicate with air traffic control, and what to do in an emergency situation. However, for most potential drone operators, especially those who are not in urban areas, these types of issues—for example, the ability to fly in crowded airspace—seemed like overkill.[72] In terms of commercial applications, the 40 required flight hours and roughly $10,000 cost limit the potential workforce.[73] Indeed, that the FAA jettisoned the idea of a pilot's license in favor of the drone "certificate" was a gesture toward the concern that the bar not be excessively high for operating a commercial drone.

A line of criticism less likely to resonate is the opposition by groups such as the AUVSI to the existing ban on commercial drones. The association reports that for every year the ban is in place the United States foregoes $10 billion in economic benefits, which comes in the form of foregone efficiencies brought about by the intersection between drones and industry such as deliveries, monitoring crops, and so on.[74] Allowing all commercial drones as a matter of policy seems highly unlikely, and the FAA defends its quite cautious approach, stating that it aims to "integrate unmanned aircraft into the busiest, most complex airspace system in the world—and to do so while we maintain our mission—protecting the safety of the American people in the air and on the ground. That is why we are taking a staged approach to the integration of these new airspace users."[75] By "staged," the FAA likely means evolutionary, with the policy trying to keep pace with changes in the technology.

Critics, however, suggest that the staged exemptions amount to an ad hoc rather than coherent policy since the FAA seems to be issuing a slow drip of exemptions that are not based on a clear decision rule but rather responses to requests, raising the prospect of making policy-by-exemption.

A last criticism addresses whether the regulations are enforceable. With about 25 incidents in which pilots encounter drones reported per month and the burgeoning individual and commercial demand for drones, actually determining which drones are flying above 400 ft., by an airport, or for commercial purposes will prove difficult. The FAA has acknowledged this difficulty and urged individual operators of drones to heed the regulations lest there be midair collisions. However, with drones being relatively low cost and bearing no risk to the operator, there may be few incentives for self-regulation. The FAA director acknowledged that this "is certainly a serious concern and it is something that I am concerned about."[76] At the end of 2014, the FAA was investigating pictures taken from a drone above the 1,005-ft.-tall Seattle Space Needle, a clear violation of the 400-ft. flight limit. The photos appear to have been taken by a Seattle ski and skateboard shop called Casual Industrees and later posted on its website. In a response to questions about the safety of flying by the Space Needle on the online forum Reddit, a spokesperson for the company said "Thank you for the warning, hopefully we (won't) get in trouble. We are claiming ignorance on that one. Enjoy the photo! Didn't know it was so risky."[77] Illegal too, they might have added.

Aside from the enforceability question, a number of court cases have actually challenged the FAA's ability to ban commercial drones. One case found that the FAA was not entitled to fine an aerial photographer who had been using a drone in Virginia to make a commercial video. The plaintiff's legal counsel claimed that the drone was equivalent to a model aircraft. The case was later overturned, reversing the earlier decision. The basis for this reversal was the claim that any aircraft taking to the skies is subject to FAA regulations by virtue of the FAA's broad definition of "aircraft," which drones fall under. This ruling is still subject to appeal. This is unlikely to be the last word in ongoing debates about the line between hobby and commercial aircraft and appropriate regulations of each.

Q. How are states regulating the use of drones?

Although the FAA regulates what is referred to as the national airspace system, a number of states have stepped up to address what they see as lacunae in the federal regulations. In particular, the use of drones for law enforcement is a matter left up to the states, and some states are deciding that the federal laws on safety and privacy do not go far enough and that they want to augment the national-level regulations.

Much as the federal regulations on drones continue to evolve in response to the emerging technology, so too are states trying to adapt to that changing technological landscape. In 2015, 45 different states debated 156 bills dealing with drone operations. Of these, 19 passed legislation and four passed resolutions, in some cases to require a study that would better understand the safety and security of using drones. Much like cell-phone-while-driving rules, many drone rules are state-specific, some are more restrictive than the federal regulations, and almost all likely to change over time. Generally, the categories of state regulations for the use of drones are as follows: 1) no additional prohibitions beyond the federal (FAA) prohibitions; 2) state laws that ban drones by private citizens; 3) state laws that ban the use of drones by law enforcement; 4) state laws that ban the use of drones by both private citizens and law enforcement.

Idaho has been the most restrictive state with its drone regulations. It is the only state that has a law restricting use by both private citizens and law enforcement and prohibiting the use of drones "to photograph or otherwise record an individual, without such individual's written consent, for the purpose of publishing or otherwise publicly disseminating such photograph or recording." It is a law that analysts at the influential Volokh Conspiracy legal blog asserted would "undoubtedly face constitutional challenges if enforced."[78] Even the ACLU concurred that Idaho's law "may violate the First Amendment by prohibiting photography or recording by drones if an individual will profit from the recording or image."[79] The ACLU goes on to say that the law would preclude a local news station to conduct a traffic report via drone "absent written consent of everyone on the road," which obviously is not required of traffic reports involving helicopters, which are frequently used to produce traffic reports.[80]

A number of states also prohibit drones by law enforcement agencies. Virginia was the first state to pass a moratorium on law enforcement drones in 2013, although by 2015 the two-year moratorium had expired and a law replaced the moratorium, allowing drones for law enforcement but only after police have acquired a warrant. Idaho, Florida, Illinois, Montana, Oregon, and Tennessee lawmakers had followed Virginia's initial anti–law enforcement drone move, with Florida passing a "Freedom from Unwarranted Surveillance Act" as to directly signal their opposition to the use of drones for surveillance.[81] The legislation mirrors the United States House of Representatives' bill, "Preserving Freedom from Unwarranted Surveillance Act of 2013," which would protect individuals against "unwarranted governmental intrusion through the use of unmanned aerial vehicles commonly called drones." The only exceptions are for those with permits, although exceptions can also occur if the Department of Homeland Security claims the presence of a terrorist threat or if there are circumstances in which "swift action" must be taken to save a life.

Many of the other states' regulations reflect cultural and political peculiarities. For example, Texas' law "is designed to protect oil pipelines from being photographed by environmentalists while allowing law enforcement agencies to do surveillance of citizens based on a legal standard that's only one step from a hunch." It also allows real estate brokers to use drones for marketing, specifically authorizes the collection of images for scholarly research, and allows surveillance on property within 25 miles of the United States border "with the consent of the individual who owns or lawfully occupies the real property captured in the image."[82] Arkansas prohibits the use of drones for voyeurism, and Mississippi designates the use of drones for "peeping Tom" activities as a felony. Arizona's legislation offers protection just for US citizens (as opposed to immigrants) against surveillance. Georgia, which has promoted the aerospace and in particular the drone industry in its state, and hosted the International Conference on Unmanned Aircraft Systems in 2013, has sought to make the state drone-friendly. As a top-five aerospace employer in 2012 eyeing the potential $10 billion drone industry with the burgeoning commercial sector, Georgia has worked to sidestep regulations that might be seen as anything but friendly to drones.[83] It passed a resolution in 2015 that established a House committee study on the safe use of drones to better incorporate and encourage drones in the state.

As the American Civil Liberties Union concludes in its analysis of state-level regulations on drones, "the legislative and public debate over drones is just getting started." A number of states currently have proposals in discussion, or have passed initial legislation, and have stopgap measures in place as they come to terms with implications of widespread drone usage and develop longer-term policies.[84]

Q. How does the regulation of nonmilitary drones vary outside the United States?

Although all countries that have contemplated the integration of drones into national airspace have expressed concern about safety and privacy, drone regulation varies quite a bit by country. As one attorney advocate for drones put it, "almost every other country in the world currently provides a more hospitable environment for UAS operations than the United States."[85] This section suggests that the statement may be exaggerated. As the United States has become more permissive with its regulations, other countries, initially more permissive, are becoming restrictive. Nonetheless, some of the initial disparity across countries seemed to present the prospect of opportunism, with companies relocating research and development to countries with less restrictive policies. Agricultural drone companies such as Indiana-based PrecisionHawk have indicated that will be investing more in Canada, South America, and Australia until commercial applications are more available in the United States, and Google and Amazon have largely done their testing outside the United States. While one argument suggests that this maintains important safety requirements, another perspective suggests that if the testing will be done anyway, it might as well remain in the United States.

Some countries such as Mexico have few to no restrictions on commercial drones. Indeed, one assessment implied that Mexican policies actually encourage drones, with the government having rewarded one young scientist for his exploration of drones. The government uses drones for drug enforcement and university research. Similarly, Brazil has not had laws specifically restricting the use of UAVs and the nation has become a popular destination for drone manufacturers, with eight in São Paulo alone.[86] Japan has likewise embraced drone technologies, having used drones for agriculture for decades. To be sure, there are differences between the nature of farming in Japan and that in the United States. As one columnist put it, "The average Japanese rice paddy, it's safe to say, is quite a bit smaller than the average Midwestern cornfield."[87] Nonetheless, AUVSI looks with envy at Japan as the model case for US commercial adoption. Once it adopted drones in 1990, Japan's rates of growth doubled in the first year and increased by 50% the following year, before tapering off as the technology became widespread across the agriculture industry.[88]

Canada has also been generally less restrictive in its regulation of drones, but mostly as a function of having been dilatory in creating policies consistent with the technology rather than being intentionally more lenient. Initially, it had considered unmanned aircraft under 77.2 lb. (35 kg) that were individually owned and not profit-seeking to be model aircraft that do not require permission to fly.[89] This quite wide latitude has left this category of aircraft relatively unregulated, despite drones actually flying faster, higher, and farther than model airplanes. As a result, the Civil Aviation Authority (CAA) proposed new rules to deal with the emerging safety risks, responding to growing concerns about the emerging and growing prevalence of the technology. Indeed, the absence of more systematic safety policies has raised red flags in Canada. One study conducted by a Canadian privacy and security group warned that since even these personal drones can be equipped with cameras, they could infringe on the privacy of Canadian citizens, and concluded that the government did not have a clear policy on those recreational drones.[90]

Transport Canada has been trying to stay apace with the emerging technology. The government issued its *Interim Approach to the Regulation of Remotely Piloted Aircraft Systems*, which was a set of proposals to be debated by the remotely piloted aircraft community. They proposed lowering the threshold for which it would regulate drones, down to 55 lb. (25 kg), as well as modifying the somewhat arbitrary distinction between recreational and non-recreational drones, while also creating a set of flight rules and evaluating the risks of individually operated drones in a more systematic way. Still, the rules governing the use of drones in Canada continue to evolve as the technology changes and proliferates. Until new rules were implemented, Transport Canada reported that it would issue exemptions to drones under 55 lb. (under 25 kg) and operating under specific conditions, including within the line of sight; otherwise, individuals require special flight operations certificates prior to use.[91] Transport Canada reports that it issued 1,672 such certificates in 2014, compared to 945 in 2013, and just 345 in 2012, an increase in 485% over two years.[92]

A number of other countries acknowledge that they are also trailing the technology in terms of policy and regulation. The CAA in the United Kingdom acknowledged that "there are no established operating guidelines" for drones, and a University of Birmingham Police Commission report called for "urgent" measures to deal with safety and privacy concerns that the pro-liferation of drones would create.[93] The CAA divides unmanned aircraft into two categories; those up to and including 44 lb. and those over 44 lb. Aircraft up to 44 lb. are considered "small unmanned aircraft," and require only a "Permit to Fly" clas-sification. This classification is fairly easy to obtain and places limits on where and at what altitude one may fly the UAV. As of September 12, 2014, 365 companies had this classification. Aircraft over 44 lb., or aircraft of any size used for aerial pho-tography, require a "Permit to Carry Out Aerial Work," which comes with more stringent restrictions, including having a qualified pilot and a certified design.[94] All drones operating in Canada are currently restricted to flying no closer than 164 ft. from a building and within the line of sight of the operator. One CAA spokesman has suggested that this line-of-sight provi-sion could be eliminated "when we see a device able to make decisions about avoiding whatever objects are out there," with operators also required to prove the safety of their devices.[95]

The European Aviation Safety Agency (EASA) allows member states to regulate drones under about 150 kg (about 330 lb.), which essentially includes almost any conceivable drone, with quite a bit of intra-Europe variation below that threshold.[96] For example, France requires that drone operators take a training course, with urban flights requiring specific government approval in advance and night-time flights prohibited. Violations face fines of 75,000 euros (about $80,000). Germany requires a special permit if the drone is heavier than 55 lb., and commercial use must be regis-tered and approved by a local aviation authority. Other countries, like Spain, have used their latitude to ban commercial drones altogether. Europe, as with Canada, has been playing catch-up when it comes to the burgeoning drone trend and recognizes that the result is a set of quite fragmented regulatory rules. To address these shortcomings, the European Commission initiated a consultation process that would culminate in a new set of safety requirements for drones which they hope would allow it to balance safety with maintaining a lead role in developing and implementing the emerging technology.

China, with about two dozen manufacturers of drones, is one of the largest players in the drone industry. According to *Aviation Week*, between 2015 and 2024, China is projected to spend 25% more on the acquisition of drones. China is also home to the Aviation Industry Corporation of China (AVIC), which is expected to lead the world in drone production by 2024, with 38.7% of the market compared to Northrop Grumman's roughly 20% and General Atomics' 10% share.[97] Chinese domestic regulations can appear both more liberal and more restrictive than other countries. On the one hand, China states that drones can be flown with permission and some American industry groups suggest that China has far surpassed the United States in this regard. As the *International Business Times* suggested, somewhat pessimistically, "it appears that the Asian nation's consumers will likely be getting their products delivered via this futuristic new version of airmail sooner than their fellow shoppers in America."[98]

On the other hand, the state appears to have granted permission to operate drones only to government groups or state-linked businesses that use drones for activities such as the surveillance of power lines and marine activity. As a legal scholar at the China University of Political Science and Law and director of the Aviation Law Committee of the Beijing Bar Association put it:

> Civilian drones face very strict regulations on the mainland. Anything that flies, like hot air balloons or drones, must have official permission. Our country is ready to go

to war. It is always on the alert for national safety threats, although in the case of commercial civilian drones, public safety is also at stake.

Several examples point to the high degree of restrictiveness in terms of operating drones in China. In one case, the efforts by a Shanghai bakery seeking to deliver desserts more quickly than ground traffic would otherwise permit saw their efforts thwarted. Low altitude airspace is heavily controlled by the Civil Aviation Administration. In a December 2013 incident, four UAV operators conducting surveillance of areas east of Beijing were arrested and detained on the grounds of a "crime of endangering public security." China mobilized more than 1,200 soldiers, 123 military vehicles, and two aircraft to track the drones.[99]

As this example suggests, regulations on civilian drones in China remain in development.[100] Shunfeng Express, a parcel delivery service referred to as the "UPS of the East," has been authorized to begin testing drone delivery to remote areas of China, using an eight-propeller drone that flies at about 328 ft. (100 m).[101] Drone operators, of whom there are an estimated 10,000 in China, are required to have a pilot's license for aircraft over 15 lb. Over 256 lb., operators must have both the pilot's license and drone certification. All flights must be approved in advance.[102]

African governments, initially permissive, are also moving toward tight regulations. Despite efforts by nongovernmental organizations to promote drones for wildlife protection, several African governments, including Kenya, have moved to ban privately owned drones mounted with cameras, citing security and privacy issues.[103] One observer lamented, "drones are supposed to help us save the rhinos and the elephants—something they're not going to be able to do if they're banned." Yet Kenya did just this, banning drones and effectively grounding major anti-poaching programs, including one spearheaded by a scientist from the University of Maryland who had come up with an algorithm that predicted, based on wildlife activity and previous poaching, where poaching was likely to occur so that a drone could intercept the poacher before animals were killed. As the scientist reported, after the ban it became "open season," as animal poaching returned to prior levels.[104]

As this section suggests, drone laws vary widely country to country, although in general the US commercial laws were initially more restrictive, creating the unintended consequence of nudging American companies such as Amazon to limit their research and development testing to indoor facilities and overseas, where drone regulations are generally looser.[105] Amazon is expected to begin delivering packages in Mumbai and Bangalore in part due to India's less stringent regulation. As the *The Economic Times* put it, India also "still hasn't woken up to the need for rules that will govern the use of unmanned aerial vehicles." For example, drone operators were not required to obtain permits for a number of drone activities that are prohibited in countries such as the United States.[106]

Google has similarly been restricted to small tests at a research facility at NASA Ames in Silicon Valley and to more extensive tests in Queensland, Australia. Here it has successfully conducted 30 delivery tests of first-aid kits, water bottles, and chocolate bars. These have all been done using prototypes of fixed-wing and rotor drones through an endeavor called Project Wing, a drone-based delivery system run by the secretive Google X team, which encountered headwinds.[107] Project Wing's aircraft had a wingspan of about 4.9 ft. (1.5 m) and was a cross between a helicopter and airplane, called a Tail Sitter because they sat on the ground with propellers up, and then would take off vertically before flying horizontally to their preprogrammed destination.[108] Google had tested the design in Australia, which as Google put it, "has a long history of allowing civilian commercial use of UAVs (drones) so we were able to do many different tests and gather some great data about our technology."[109] Australia does require that aircraft be operated in daytime, not through clouds or fog, and away from heavily populated areas, but conditions in the country are conducive to that. Through a series of tests, Google X discovered design flaws, and planned to test a new design platform, also in Australia.

Although FAA rules have been more restrictive than policies elsewhere, they have also been also under more pressure from the industry to liberalize their commercial drone policies. Compared to the 167 requests for exemption that the FAA received as of 2014, its European counterpart had had only one such request, an Airbus designed to do surveillance of oil pipes, railways, and disaster response.[110] The pressure from industry in the United States, even if approvals were given on a case-by-case basis, could produce faster integration of commercial drones compared with Europe, where "the lack of industry pressure compared with the United States could drag the process even longer."[111]

6

THE FUTURE OF DRONES

NANO, AUTONOMOUS SYSTEMS, AND SCIENCE FICTION

The next phase of development in unmanned technologies is likely to take place in micro/nanoscale technologies or autonomous systems, both of which stand to change the way drones are used and which each present a new set of debates. As *Vice* puts it, "in keeping with its vision for a 'smaller and leaner' military that's agile, flexible, fast, and cutting-edge, the DoD will work on 'miniaturizing' drones and drone weapons to make them smaller, lighter and less energy-consuming." That comment draws on the Defense Department's 25-year Unmanned Roadmap, which observes that by going in the direction of miniaturization, it will also make the systems more affordable for the US taxpayer.[1]

All of these capture the imagination and are increasingly portrayed in science fiction, from movies to video games to books. This concluding chapter first investigates the turn to miniaturization and then closes with prognostications about the future of drones, and whether the future will look more like a science fiction movie or whether science fiction involving drones will be mere escapism, with life ultimately not imitating art.

Q. What is the future of drone hardware?

During the 2015 Consumer Electronics Show (CES) in Law Vegas, one technology analyst observed that "drones are arguably the most hyped product at CES."[2] As this book has suggested, militaries are increasingly relying on drones, as are state governments, hobbyists, relief organizations, and industry. Strong and apparently enduring interest in drones is likely to push big technological advancements; the question is in which direction. Certainly there are the more incremental developments such as selfie-taking drones, but at least in terms of the platforms themselves, the more significant moves are toward smaller, lighter drones and more capacious, stealthy military drones.

One important move for drone technology is toward miniaturization, leveraging smaller and lighter technologies that, when combined with unmanned systems, can mean more effective surveillance and reconnaissance without detection. This has important battlefield utility for soldiers who seek to identify threats over a hill without themselves being in the line of fire, among other examples. The size and stealth advantage, however, also makes mini-drones difficult to regulate or defend, as the technology will be too small to be controlled or picked up by air defenses.

If the Federal Aviation Administration relaxes some of its drone regulations, estimates suggest that 15,000 drones will fly in US airspace by 2020 and 30,000 by 2030.[3] Many of these drones will likely be very small (mini- or insect drones), following the move of industry, universities, and the military toward miniaturization. In addition to the individual images that these drones can produce is the potential for working together in swarms that can fly together in some type of formation and create a composite picture of a particular environment.

Most of the current miniature drones fit broadly under the heading of micro- or mini-drones, which are characterized at least by the Pentagon as under 20 lb., though with many much lighter than that. The Raven, a small hand-launched unmanned aerial vehicle made by AeroVironment, is neither particularly small nor light, with a 4.6-foot wingspan and a 4.2-lb. weight. The Raven was able to project pictures from 15,000 ft., which led to their popularity and a production run of about 19,000.[4] The next step in miniaturization is to go smaller than the Raven. Much as the maritime drones have borrowed from nature by leveraging animals such as fish, shark, and eels, micro-aerial vehicles tend to have "biological inspiration" in the form of flies and insects.[5] As the Air Force Research Lab suggests, the objective is to mimic nature in order to "hide in plain sight"[6] the implication being that these vehicles would look like insects but actually be conducting surveillance or collecting images. These aircraft tend to have shorter battery life and range, but have the advantage of entering locations that would be inaccessible to other forms of aerial surveillance.

One of the first such micro-drones was the T-Hawk, short for Tarantula Hawk—a type of wasp. The T-Hawk has a vertical takeoff and landing ability and the ability to hover and stare, allowing it to identify and monitor IEDs, do battle damage assessment, and carry out homeland security operations, all while fitting in a backpack. It was used to conduct surveillance after the Fukushima nuclear power accident in Japan in 2011. The T-Hawk carried out operations that would have been dangerous for humans because of radiation exposure. Since the T-Hawk is not susceptible to radioactive exposure, it could take imagery of the reactor to assess the origins from which radioactivity was emanating.[7]

The TechJect Dragonfly, another micro-drone, this is the product of researchers at Georgia Tech, who were aided by a $1 million grant from the US Air Force. The Dragonfly is roughly 6 in. long and weighs about .88 oz. It is able to hover for 8–10 minutes or perform a combination of hovering and fixed-wing flying for 25–30 minutes. The Dragonfly carries up to 20 sensors, which allow it to take pictures and perform reconnaissance. Depending on the model, the Dragonfly would retail anywhere from $250 to $1,500.[8]

Another example is AeroVironment's Hummingbird drone, funded by the Defense Advanced Research Projects Agency

(DARPA), which was developed to maneuver much like a hummingbird after which it is named. It has a 6.5-in. wingspan and weighs about 0.67 ounces (19 g), making it only slightly larger than the average hummingbird. The drone is also able to perch on objects, such as a window ledge, and gather intelligence about its target via its built-in audio and video recorders. Hummingbird drones could also be used to locate survivors in rubble and investigate locations where there are potentially hazardous chemicals.[9]

The Black Hornet Nano was developed by a Norwegian company, Prox Dynamics, and is currently being used by the British Army. The Black Hornet is 4 in. long and weighs .67 oz. It is well suited to reconnaissance, as it flies nearly silently and is colored to blend in with the grey mud buildings that are common in many Afghan villages. The drone captures video and still images, which it can send to a handheld terminal up to 3,280 ft. (1,000 m) away. The Black Hornet is able to be directly controlled by a pilot or to operate autonomously using global positioning system (GPS).[10]

What makes these technologies fascinating is not only their small size but also their resemblance to actual insects. Figure 6.1 shows a RoboBee, designed in the Harvard University Robotics Laboratory, whose wings gyrate similar to those of an insect and which is smaller than a penny.[11] In 2012, a graduate student demonstrated that the RoboBee could ascend into the air, hover, and carry out controlled flight maneuvers. In his review of micro-drone technology, Adam Piore writes that "until recently, inventors lacked the aerodynamics expertise to turn diagrams into mechanical versions of something as quotidian as a fly or a bee."[12]

With these nano-drones though, questions about privacy become even more salient. These drones, because they resemble insects so closely, can truly hide in plain sight. What could seem like a fly might actually have sensors and small cameras. Google's executive chairman, Eric Schmidt, expressed concern about the privacy issues of small drones that fly into

Figure 6.1 Harvard Microbotics Lab

a neighbor's backyard, but also those that could be used as terrorist weapons, sneaking into high casualty areas and doing maximum damage.[13] His recommendation included an international treaty that would regulate inexpensive nano-drones. "It's got to be regulated. You just can't imagine that British people would allow this sort of thing, and I can't imagine American people would allow this sort of thing. It's one thing for governments, who have some legitimacy in what they're doing, but have other people doing it.... It's not going to happen."[14] The nano-drone might not be equipped to carry out the damage, at least in terms of security and terrorism, that Schmidt outlines, but he is not the first to raise these privacy concerns. Another observer put it, with the introduction of the Zano, a personal nano-drone, "the personal paparazzi nano drone has arrived."[15]

While miniaturization is one significant advance for the future of drones, another end of the developmental continuum is toward faster, stealthier, more capacious military drones. The most sophisticated armed drone has been the Reaper, which remains quite vulnerable even to a rudimentary set of air defense systems. The next wave of advancements is likely to come in the form of faster, stealthier, less vulnerable drones. In some of its most ambitious plans, the Pentagon envisions a long-range strike bomber that can flip a switch and transform from a manned aircraft to one that is unmanned and flown remotely. As an optimistic interpretation, this vision would be the best of both worlds, bringing the advantages of unmanned and manned aircraft: the combination of little risk to pilots and long-enduring missions that loiter, which comes with unmanned aircraft, with the flexibility and ability to make quick decisions about rapidly changing security environments, attributes of manned platforms. The former vice chairman of the Joint Chiefs of Staff, General Cartwright, argued that while there are psychological hang-ups about using unmanned bombers to deliver nuclear weapons, intercontinental ballistic missiles are also unmanned, though the ambitious vision would allow nuclear weapons to be delivered in the manned mode of the next-generation bomber.[16] A less sanguine interpretation would point to previous military efforts to produce multirole platforms, including the F-35, and the tendency for enormous cost overruns in the effort to be all things to all people (or services).

Even farther on the horizon is the idea of a combat drone that can engage in dogfights, which are the type of air-to-air combat missions that were common in World War II when, for example, the German Luftwaffe would shoot down Russian aircraft, and that popularized by the movie *Top Gun*. While this type of combat is becoming less and less frequent, with stand-off weapons reducing the need for these maneuvers, the experimental X-47B unmanned combat air vehicle program has toyed with the idea of a future dogfight capability. Until now, this capability has been elusive. On December 23, 2002, during the American effort to depose Saddam Hussein, an Predator drone of the United States Air Force fired a Stinger missile at an Iraqi MiG-25. These air-to-air missiles had been attached to the drone's airframe in what can only be called a haphazard effort to defend the aircraft against aerial threats.

Indeed, the Stinger missile did not hit the Iraqi aircraft, which subsequently shot the drone out of the sky. While this lopsided engagement could hardly be called a success story of unmanned flight, it was nonetheless significant in that it was the first time a drone had done battle with a manned counterpart.

The possibility of unmanned dogfighters presents numerous advantages. The most obvious advantage to such a system is that aircraft loss would not incur any human cost. Furthermore, a drone is not hindered by the limitations posed by having a human on board: not only would such an aircraft not require support systems such as an oxygen supply and a cockpit, but it would also be unhindered by the G-force limitations of the human body. Such a drone would thus be able to execute high-G maneuvers, a crucial component of dogfights, without knocking out or killing its pilot. Furthermore, if militaries are leery of phasing out the fighter pilot for drones, these dogfighting-capable drones craft could perform admirably as a complement to manned air superiority fighters, either as robotic wingmen or simply as cannon fodder. The efficacy of the drone in the latter role was dramatically demonstrated during the Yom Kippur War, when Israel used unarmed drones to force Egypt to expend its arsenal of anti-air missiles. The Israeli Air Force subsequently exploited Egypt's vulnerability. It was postulated that such a tactic could be employed by the Soviet Union against American aircraft carriers patrolling the Pacific.

In spite of the potential benefits associated with air superiority drones, little tangible progress has been made toward fielding one. America's current fleet of drones is dominated by "hunter-killer" drones such as the Predator and Reaper, both of which serve in surveillance and air-to-ground roles. Neither the Predator nor Reaper is sufficiently aerodynamic to meet the rigorous demands of air combat.

As previously mentioned, the closest any military has come to actually developing an unmanned dogfighter involves plans for the American Navy's UCLASS aircraft. As a carrier-capable drone, the UCLASS could be equipped with missiles able to conduct air-to-air strikes. Another possibility is the conversion of a pre-existing manned aircraft into a drone. The United States Air Force has already converted the Korean War-era F-86 Sabre and the Vietnam-era F-4 into target drones for training purposes. More interestingly, a 4th-generation F-16 Falcon was converted into an unmanned platform. During testing, the drone, dubbed the QF-16, successfully completed 9-G maneuvers typical of those required during dogfights. The possibility of converting manned air systems to drones in an effort to reduce the human toll of air wars could serve a valuable function.

Given the potential unmanned aerial systems have for air combat, and given the degree to which the United States military has incorporated UAV's in recent military operations, it may seem incongruous for such little progress to have been made in the development of unmanned fighters. One of the principal setbacks to such an enterprise has been cost: the United States has dedicated a substantial amount of resources to the development of its 5th-generation manned fighters such as the F-35 or F-22. Furthermore, the fact remains that the United States Air Force has been dominated by manned aircraft since the end of World War II. The fighter pilot is a revered figure in military circles, and is unlikely to be phased out without extreme reluctance. While unmanned dogfights are unlikely in the near future, as drones become a more integral part of the military, a serious conversation about the future of the manned dogfighter will likely be taking place.

Q. What is the future of autonomy?

The move toward miniaturization on the one hand and sophisticated, nuclear-capable, dogfighting combat drones on the other both speak to advances in hardware. Another set of developments is taking place in the area of software, in particular in the direction of autonomy. Autonomous systems are just as the name implies: technologies that have been programmed and operate without remote piloting. They can be used for many of the same purposes as semiautonomous systems and with perhaps a greater range will come to include cars and space vehicles. These systems do introduce a different set of technical challenges since more sensitive and nuanced sensors are required to anticipate and control situations such as landing, targeting, or navigating. They also have triggered considerable skepticism about the implications of altogether removing humans from military decision-making.

In 2013, the Pentagon issued a roadmap that spelled out its 25-year vision for drones, with bullet points highlighting the hope that it would "take the 'man' out of 'unmanned'" through greater automation of its drones. Its hope is to create higher levels of autonomy and move away from the high level of human control that characterizes the current technology.[17] At the same time, the military expresses wariness about full automation in the following way:

> For a significant period into the future, the decision to pull the trigger or launch a missile from an unmanned system will not be fully automated, but it will remain under the full control of a human operator. Many aspects of the firing sequence will be fully automated but the decision to fire will not likely be fully automated until legal, rules of engagement, and safety concerns have all been thoroughly examined and resolved.[18]

That the Pentagon believes that these legal questions could be resolved points to the expectation that at some point we will live in a fully automated world, even in the realm of targeting. As the section on international law suggests, decisions about combatants versus civilians are inherently fraught, especially in environments where civilians routinely traverse into combatant status and back and where the definition of "direct participation in hostilities" can be quite ambiguous. Technology may be able to provide better intelligence but is unlikely to be better at adjudicating subjective and inherently philosophical questions of where indirect participation ends and direct participation begins.[19] The statement that automation will only result under those conditions either underestimates those philosophical or fully appreciates those challenges, in which case fully automated systems will remain science fiction.

Some roboticists are trying to tackle this problem by equipping machines with a moral compass, an "ethical adapter," that can generate a sense of compassion when faced with the prospect of lethal force. The ethical adapter also tries to inculcate an "after-action reflection," which means the robot can then try to modify its future behavior based on what it learned from the previous event (including error). Another emotion that roboticists are trying to generate is one of guilt, wherein if "specific affective threshold values are exceeded, the system will cease being able to deploy lethality partially or in totality."[20] To put it mildly, as Philip Alston, former UN Special Rapporteur on extrajudicial, summary or arbitrary executions, did, "the notion that the laws of war can be reduced to programmable formulae and the idea that the human conscience can be mechanically replicated are both far more problematic than Arkin's work would suggest." Robert Arkin, who studies artificial intelligence (AI), asserts that ultimately the ethical adapter on an autonomous system can ultimately reduce civilian casualties compared to their human counterparts.[21]

In response to these potential developments, a transnational movement has mobilized to prevent the use of systems that engage targets and acquire situational awareness in the absence of human intervention. This is a form of AI that Arkin describes in his book. AI makes judgments with no human guidance after its coordinates and objectives are programmed. One movement named the Campaign to Stop Killer

Robots questions the basic premise that fully autonomous systems can function ethically and of their own accord. The group was launched in April 2013 by Jody Williams, who was also responsible for the movement that culminated in the Ottawa and Oslo Treaties that banned land mines and cluster munitions, and has proposed a ban on fully autonomous weapons. It works through the mobilization of states, which have then worked within the Convention on Conventional Weapons (CCW) to create a treaty that would preemptively ban additional development and use of these systems.[22] In November 2014, countries involved in the CCW agreed to continue to a second round of discussion about lethal autonomous weapons systems, which Human Rights Watch Arms Advocacy Director and Campaign to Stop Killer Robots Coordinator Mary Wareham cited as an acknowledgement of the importance of the topic; she also, however, cautioned that "the technology is moving faster than the international response."[23]

More recently, the CEO of electric car maker Tesla, Elon Musk, joined forces with scientist Stephen Hawking and Apple cofounder Steve Wozniak to write an open letter about the potential consequences of autonomous weapons. The letter built on Hawking's and Musk's previous cautions about AI, warning that there might be unintended consequences of greater automation since machines might not be able to understand the good and bad effects of the actions they take. The letter states that "if any major military power pushes ahead with AI weapon development, a global arms race is virtually inevitable. . . autonomous weapons are ideal for tasks such as assassinations, destabilizing nations, subduing populations, and selectively killing a particular ethic group," meaning that the proliferation of this technology would be a dangerous development.[24]

The anti-autonomy movement has found a number of allies moving the discussion forward, but some observers urge caution in taking the ban too far, risking that the proverbial baby is thrown out with the bath water. If the movement bans

precision weapons, such as the US long-range anti-ship missile and Norway's Joint Strike Missiles, which are more like
precision weapons than they are autonomous weapons, "one
of the most significant developments in the twentieth century
toward making warfare more humane and reducing civilian
casualties" will come to a halt according to Michael Horowitz
and Paul Scharre. These authors note that compared to the 50/
50 chance of bombs landing within 1.25 miles of their target
in World II, some precision munitions are accurate to 5 ft.,
which reduces the likelihood of hitting unintended targets.
Nonetheless, they too agree that fully autonomous systems
"do raise serious issues worthy of further debate."[25]

Autonomous technologies, potentially quite problematic
in armed conflict circumstances, are less likely to prove controversial in terms of civilian applications. As the *New York
Times* suggested in a review of ethics and robots, "the favor-
ite example of an ethical, autonomous robot is the driverless
car, which is still in the prototype stage at Google and other
companies."[26] They are thought to be consistently safe compared to the often-multitasking and sometimes-competitive
human drivers. These technologies are also the basis of many
of the tests being done by Amazon and Google or by delivery
companies that program an address, for example, to which
the drone uses GPS to reach and then flies back. Project Wing,
the Google X test project seeking to enable drone-delivery
services, is intended to be autonomous, though still requires
human intervention to direct the drone around birds, weather,
and trees. The founder of Project Wing acknowledged that the
idea of doing autonomous delivery is "years from a product,
but it is the first prototype that we want to stand behind."[27]

Q. Is life imitating art or art imitating life when it comes to drones?

Science fiction media has long been a home for new and
advanced technology, and made predictions about the future

use of technology. Of course, the movie *Back to the Future II*, released in the 1980s, made a number of erroneous predictions about what life would look like in 2015. One of the memorable visions was of a world full of flying cars. The *Hollywood Reporter* described one of the missed predictions: "it's 2015, and sadly, we still need roads."[28] But the integration of drones into popular culture is a less far-fetched proposition since they are already a feature of conflict, commercial, and civilian life. Indeed, drones have increasingly featured in everything from movies to video games to books.

In terms of film, popular culture quickly adopted the theme of drones. Few if any are truly science fiction, the only one being *Skyline* (2010), which portrays aliens invading Earth, the US Air Force using drones to attack a spaceship hovering over Los Angeles, and one of the drones firing a nuclear weapon at the ship. Most of the films imitate some aspect of the American use of drones in the years after 9/11. Keeping in mind that the United States was quite quietly using drones in Afghanistan beginning in November 2001, and that its first strike outside a hot battlefield was in 2002, with no additional strikes until Pakistan in 2004, the 2005 introduction of drones into film reflects Hollywood's attentiveness to what were then subtle changes on the battlefield. Ironically, the first film to portray drones did so with a multirole carrier-based Navy drone which the Navy still has not developed. The movie was *Stealth*, in which the Navy creates a combat drone controlled by AI. The project goes awry when lightning strikes the drone, which causes it to go rogue. In the end, human pilots on the aircraft carrier must destroy the drone before it engages in more rogue attacks that would incite a world war. Film critic Roger Ebert declared that the plot defied logic, only in part because the drone-related aspects of the film were outlandish, but mostly because of other implausible aspects of the film, including that one of Navy officers crosses the Korean Demilitarized Zone and that the "North Koreans have neglected to plant land mines in the part of the DMZ that Wade must cross."[29]

More plausible and indeed successful was *Mission Impossible 3*, in which drones play a somewhat minor role when foreign mercenaries use a drone to attack Ethan Hunt (Tom Cruise) and his team, allowing the mercenaries to extract Davian, who had captured Ethan. Drones were also portrayed in combat missions in several other movies, including most prominently in *Syriana* (2005), where the CIA used a Predator to assassinate the foreign minister of a recalcitrant emirate; the *Bourne Legacy* (2012), in which a CIA drone attacks the protagonist; *Eagle Eye* (2008), in which a Reaper is hijacked by a supercomputer attempting to eliminate the executive branch and the drone fires multiple missiles at the protagonist during a chase in downtown Washington before its subsequent destruction; *Hummingbird* (2013), in which the protagonist, an antihero and former soldier, is spotted and possibly killed by a British drone; and *Furious 7* (2015), in which a drone is deployed over Los Angeles by the movie's antagonist to pursue and destroy the protagonists' vehicles. All of these films involve a similar plotline, which is the use of drones commanded or commandeered to strike targets. The next *Top Gun* movie takes drone operations to the next level, where Tom Cruise engages in dogfights with combat drones, which has not yet actually been a feature of contemporary conflict but likely will be in the future.

A handful of films have involved the ethical and psychological aspects of drones. *From the Sky* (2014) is a short film about an Arab father and son who travel through an area frequently targeted by US drones. The father suffers from posttraumatic stress disorder (PTSD) due to the drone strikes. In *The Other Side* (2014), a Pakistani boy observes American drone strikes in his neighborhood and subsequently joins a terrorist group. Picking up this theme of how strikes in places such as Pakistan have had ripple effects, *Four Lions* (2010) portrays four incompetent British jihadists traveling to a training camp in Pakistan, where they unsuccessfully attempt to shoot down an American drone. *Good Kill* (2014) takes the perspective of the drone operator himself, as it focuses on an American Air Force pilot who questions the morality of his job in the face of the vast degree of collateral damage caused by his missions. Two films address the domestic legality of drone policy. While *The Giver* (2014) shows drones are used by the government to monitor citizens and report acts of wrongdoing, *Robocop* (2014), the 2014 remake of the original 1987 film, acknowledges the legality of combat drones abroad but cites the fictional Dreyfus Act, which prevents domestic use of combat drones.

While film has been the most visible media form to involve drones, other media forms have joined in. In terms of television, the 2014 season of the show *24: Live Another Day* centered on American drones, including one hijacked by a terrorist and used to attack London, and one episode of the popular show *Homeland* focused on an accidental CIA drone strike on a wedding party in Pakistan, quite closely mirroring an actual strike that occurred in Yemen.

Video games have also gotten in on the action. The whole *Call of Duty* franchise involves some aspect of drones, and Predator drones are frequently mentioned and deployed. *Call of Duty: Black Ops 2* includes American drones hijacked by a terrorist organization and used to attack China, a plot that bears resemblance to the show 24 discussed above. Books have increasingly drawn on drone imagery as well. Many of Tom Clancy's recent books involve drones. For example, in *Threat Vector*, China hacks into American military networks and disables the country's drone arsenal. Peter Singer, who has written nonfiction involving drones, has also written fiction, including a book called *Ghost Fleet* that is part science fiction and part fact, bringing together military fact in the form of stealth drones, cyberwar, and insurgency but also fiction in the form of space pirates. Lastly, former counterterrorism czar Richard Clarke infuses his foreign policy expertise into a book called *Sting of the Drone*, in which a Pakistan-based terrorist group hacks into Predator drones based on Creech Air Force Base and uses them against the US government.

Science fiction has long integrated futuristic robotics into its images, with Isaac Asimov being among the first to popularize the futuristic technology with his robot short stories that he began writing in 1939. More recent popular culture has done more to reflect on the current applications than imagine those of the future, and has tried to take stock of the potential privacy, legal, and psychological implications of how drones have proliferated. In this respect, off-Broadway plays such as *Grounded*, which is a one-person drama that gets into the minds of a conflicted drone operator who goes to 12-hour shifts in an Air Force trailer and wrestles with the intimacy of seeing targets nearly side-by-side with her own family, captures many of the ongoing debates about the use of drones more generally.

Q. Are drones here to stay?

The world is becoming awash with drones and the indications are that these are not only here to stay, but will spread, within militaries, in the commercial sphere, and for recreational uses. The questions are then what that world of drones looks like and how to craft it in ways that balance concerns about industrial capacity with those of safety, privacy, and international and regional security. The universe of possible applications, as earlier sections have indicated, is nearly endless, and observers are lining up to prognosticate about the direction drones will go.

Soon after Amazon revealed that it had requested to test drones for delivering packages, the *Guardian* crafted the following thought exercise to prompt readers to consider the future of drones:

It is Glastonbury 2024, and you've got a front-row spot for the headline act, the Rolling Stones, concluding their fifth farewell tour. You need a drink badly, so you get out your smartphone and dial up a drone, which within minutes delivers a plastic bottle from the bar a mile away.

Glastonbury, of course, is a major outdoor festival in the southwest of England, the English version of Woodstock. The vignette presents a scenario where obtaining a beverage while maintaining one's position can be a challenge—and the prospect of a drone delivery can seem quite appealing. The effort to deliver beer by drone has floundered in the United States, not just because of the prohibition against commercial drones but also the fundamental concerns about "possible careless and reckless operation, especially if someone on the ground is hurt by an object or objects falling from the UAVs," according to a Federal Aviation Administration (FAA) spokesman, a position that for the moment halts any potential deliveries of six-packs via drone.[30]

The idea, however, is not outside the realm of possibility. While some software applications such as Snapchat have been derided as a technology on which an economy cannot depend,[31] the flipside may be that "hardware is becoming the new software,"[32] and tech firms are now turning their eye away from software and toward hardware. The reason is that many of the world's most serious problems, which do not include rapid delivery of beer, can be addressed through innovation in hardware and not software. One San Francisco venture capital fund specializing in revolutionary technology adopted the saying: "we wanted flying cars, instead we got 140 characters." Investments have increasingly flowed into hardware, whether small-scale nuclear reactors, 3D printers, and, yes, drones. Industrial and energy startups attracted $1.24 billion in venture capital for the first half of 2014, twice as much as compared to the same time a year earlier.[33] Silicon Valley committed $95 million to drone startups between 2013 and 2014. One of these companies, Skydio, aims "to build true computer vision into drones, enabling them to navigate based not on GPS but on what they 'see.'"[34] The company is the brainchild of a group of individuals who met at the Massachusetts Institute of Technology (MIT) and were part of the founding team of Google X's Project Wing. The technology would help

drones "sense and avoid collisions," one of the key impediments to broader integration of commercial drones into the
national airspace given the potential for drones to collide with
manned aircraft.[35] One of the cofounders explained that "the
goal is to take something that normally costs $5,000 and sell it
for $50." Lowering the cost of entry would lower the barriers
for more individuals who are not willing to spend thousands
of dollars on drone technology.[36]

The increased interest and development in hardware such as
drones, however, will only be as fruitful as the regulatory environment allows it to become. Even hobbyist drones, not currently
regulated when they fly under 400 ft., weigh less than 55 lb., and
are not used for commercial purposes, have come under scrutiny. Exemplified by the security concerns elicited by a drone-
enthusiast government bureaucrat landing a hobby drone on
the lawn of the White House, both the government and populace seem increasingly leery of even small quadcopters carrying
explosives and being used for terrorism or assassination.

The upshot may be self-regulation, in which drone producers themselves regulate how their drones can be used. The
Chinese firm DJI, which has controlled more than 70% of the
global market in consumer drones and is the producer of the
Phantom that landed on the White House lawn, created a software update that prevents its drones from flying in particular
areas (in this case the White House), which is referred to as
geofencing. Already, DJI had added no-fly-zone firmware to its
drones, whereby a flight within five miles of a major airport
causes the maximum altitude of the aircraft to drop and the
drone to land and then refuse to take off again. While some hobbyists were not pleased about the geofencing limitations, the
firm itself has incentives to have their technology flown safely,
as rampant, reckless use only intensifies interest in greater regulation, which would likely impede sales of drones.[37]

Beyond self-regulation, the federal government also
appears to be interested in the regulation of this category of
drones. In its November 2014 Notice of Proposed Rulemaking

(NPRM), the FAA announced a tentative set of regulations for all small unmanned aerial systems, including operating standards for model aircraft and low performance (e.g., toy) operations, to increase the safety and efficiency of the National Air Space (NAS). These proposed rules preceded the incident involving a toy drone on the White House but certainly speak to the concerns about how even small drones can have large impacts.[38]

The attention to small drones is consistent with increasing concern among the public about lightweight drones. In a January 2015 *Reuters* poll, about 73% of Americans expressed an interest in greater regulations for small, privately owned drones. Among those surveyed, 42% (a plurality) opposed private drone ownership altogether, 30% approved, and another 28% were unsure. This poll also preceded the incident involving the drone on the White House grounds.[39] In a separate question within the same poll, 64% were opposed to their neighbor having a drone, though 68% of individuals were supportive of the police having drones for certain types of law enforcement.

Speaking to the concerns about privacy, the private sector has stepped in and established something akin to the "no-call list," but for drones. NoFlyZone is a company with whom individuals register their address and that in turn prohibits where private drones can fly. The company essentially operates a database that helps regulate where drones are used in part so that the public is more comfortable with private drones in ways that allows them to continue to develop without federally imposed prohibitions. Unlike the DJI firmware, which does not apply to drones already sold since these do not connect to the Internet, NoFlyZone enables a cloud-based system that makes partnership with drone operating system producers such as DroneDeploy and PixiePath attractive. As Atherton writes, "if NoFlyZone takes off, people can register to keep their homes free of hostile intruders," an "opt-in alternative for individuals who wish to protect their own privacy, without the need for an FAA mandate."[40]

As these developments suggest, the technology has largely led the policy on drones. This is not entirely surprising since the technology has come of age in a short period of time, from just a blip on a development radar in the 1990s to the major feature of US counterterrorism strategy soon after the 9/11 attacks, and now one of the most sought-after holiday presents around. As the book has implied, the introduction of drones presents both opportunities and concerns, which helps sketch out the two possible future worlds. One future is a world in which individual concerns about safety and privacy prompt governments to impose strict regulations on commercial and individual applications. This would be a world with few drones and a failed prognostication about the ubiquity of drones, much as *Back to the Future* misread a future of flying cars. Another future is a world where individuals, industry, and government embrace the new technology and Amazon's CEO Jeff Bezos will have been accurate in predicting that drones would be "as common as seeing a mail truck."[41] One thing is for sure. Even if not ubiquitous, drones are here to stay.

NOTES

Foreword

1. Chris Woods, "Ten Years Since First Deadly Drone Strike, Industry Gathers in London," *The Bureau of Investigative Journalism*, November 21, 2011.

Chapter 1

1. Bart Elias, *Pilotless Drones: Background and Considerations for Congress Regarding Unmanned Aircraft Operations in the National Airspace System*, US Congressional Research Service, 2012.
2. Robert Johnson, "FAA: Look for 30,000 Drones to Fill American Skies by the End of the Decade," *Business Insider*, February 8, 2012.
3. Nick Wingfield, "New FAA Report Tallies Drone Sightings, Highlighting Safety Issues," *New York Times*, November 26, 2014.
4. Miranda Green, "On the Home Front, Drones Are Quickly Shot Down by States," *Daily Beast*, March 9, 2013.
5. Chris Anderson, "Relatively Cheap Drones with Advanced Sensors and Imaging Capabilities Are Giving Farmers New Ways to Increase Yields and Reduce Crop Damage," *Technology Review,* available at http://www.technologyreview.com/featuredstory/526491/agricultural-drones/.
6. "GoPro Inc's Consumer Drones Could Help Its Stock Take Off," *NASDAQ* December 2, 2014, available at http://tealgroup.com/index.php/about-teal-group-corporation/media/item/gopro-inc-s-consumer-drones-could-help-its-stock-take-off.
7. Ben Popper, "The Drone You Should Buy Right Now," *The Verge*, July 31, 2014.

8. Brian Merchant, "The Best Drones Money Can Buy," *Vice*, January 13, 2014.

9. Abby Ohlheiser, "Pope Francis Has a Drone of His Very Own," *Washington Post*, April 30, 2015.

10. David Swindell, Kevin Desouza, and Sabrina PK Glimcher, "Drones and the 'Wild West' of Regulatory Experimentation," *Brookings Institution*, 17 August 2015.

11. Glennon Harrison, *Unmanned Aircraft Systems: Manufacturing Trends*, Congressional Research Service, January 2013, 2.

12. Teal Group, *World UAV Systems 2012*.

13. "Remarks by the President at the National Defense University," May 23, 2013, available at http://www.whitehouse.gov/the-press-office/2013/05/23/remarks-president-national-defense-university.

14. Zachary Keck, "Russia's Coming Combat Drones," *The Diplomat*, June 24, 2014.

15. *Unmanned Systems Integrated Roadmap: FY2013–2038*, page 3, US Department of Defense, 14-S-0553.

Chapter 2

1. Kelsey Atherton, "Flying Robots 101: Everything You Need to Know about Drones," *Popular Science*, March 7, 2013.

2. Canadian safety regulations, available at http://wwwapps.tc.gc.ca/Saf-Sec-Sur/2/NPA-APM/doc.aspx?id=10293.

3. *Unmanned Aircraft Systems Roadmap 2005–2030*, United States Department of Defense, 2005, 1.

4. Joseph Angelo, *Robotics: A Reference Guide to the New Technology*, 147.

5. *Scientific American*, March 1849.

6. Chris Cole, "Rise of the Reapers: A Brief History of Drones," available at http://dronewars.net/2014/10/06/rise-of-the-reapers-a-brief-history-of-drones/.

7. Jefferson Morley, "Israel's Drone Dominance," *Salon*, May 15, 2012.

8. "Treaty between the United States of America and the Union of Soviet Socialist Republics on the Elimination of Their Intermediate-Range and Shorter-Range Missiles," December 8, 1987.

9. Author's correspondence with retired US Air Force officer Colonel Kurt Klingenberger, January 16, 2015.

10. Michael Hastings, "The Rise of the Killer Drones: How America Goes to War in Secret," *Rolling Stone*, April 16, 2012.

11. Data from the NAF.

12. Alice Ross, "Civilian Drone Deaths Triple in Afghanistan, UN Agency Finds," BIJ, February 8, 2014.

13. Lynn Davis, Michael McNerney, James Chow, Thomas Hamilton, Sarah Harting, and Dan Byman, *Armed and Dangerous: UAVs and U.S. Security* (Rand Corporation, 2014), 9.

14. *Nonproliferation: Agencies Could Improve Information Sharing and End-Use Monitoring on Unmanned Aerial Vehicle Exports.* United States Government Accountability Office, July 2012.

15. Stephen Trimble, "Missed Targets Prompt US Marine Corps to Arm Unmanned Shadows," *FlightGlobal*, January 12, 2012.

16. L. Davis, M. McNerney, J. Chow, T. Hamilton, S. Harting, and D. Byman. "Armed and Dangerous," *RAND Corporation*, 2014.

17. Michael Horowitz and Matthew Fuhrmann, *Droning On*, unpublished manuscript.

18. General Accountability Office, *Nonproliferation: Agencies Could Improve Information Sharing and End-Use Monitoring on Unmanned Aerial Vehicle Exports*, July 2012, available at http://www.gao.gov/assets/600/593131.pdf.

19. Chris Cole, "Israel and the Drone Wars," available at *dronewarsuk. files.wordpress.com/2014/01/israel-and-the-drone-wars.pdf.*

20. Amira Haas, "Clearing the Fog on Israeli Drone Use in Gaza," *Haaretz*, March 1, 2014.

21. "Did an Israeli Drone Strike Militants in Egypt?" *Al Monitor*, August 5, 2014.

22. "UK Drone Strike Stats," available at http://dronewars.net/uk-drone-strike-list-2/.

23. Phil Stewart and Yara Bayoumy, "As Easy Targets Thin, Syria Air Strikes by US Allies Plunge," *Reuters*, December 17, 2014.

24. Eric Schmitt "Obstacles Limit Targets and Pace of Strikes on ISIS," *New York Times*, November 9, 2014.

25. Sarah Kreps, "Obama's Report Card on Drone Policy Reform," *The Hill*, May 19, 2014.

26. Scott Shane, "Debate Aside, Number of Drone Strikes Drops Sharply," *New York Times*, May 21, 2013.

27. Micah Zenko, "America Just Launched Its 500th Drone Strike," *The Atlantic*, November 21, 2014.

28. Micah Zenko, "US Transparency and the Truth of Targeted Killings," CFR.org, September 5, 2014.

29. The BIJ does not report militant numbers but rather total and civilian numbers. If one does not take into account unknown

(which BIJ does not report), then we might infer that total fatalities – civilian = militant.

30. Ritika Singh, "Drone Strikes Kill Innocent People: Why Is It So Hard to Know How Many?" *New Republic*, October 25, 2013.

31. Larry Lewis and Sarah Holewinski, "Changing of the Guard: Civilian Protection for an Evolving Military," *PRISM*, Vol. 4, No. 2 (2013): 57–66.

32. Department of Justice White Paper, "Lawfulness of a Lethal Operation Directed against a US Citizen Who Is a Senior Operational Leader of Al-Qa'ida or an Associated Force."

33. Scott Neuman, "Man Accused in 1998 Bombings of US Embassies Dies in Custody," *NPR*, January 3, 2015.

34. Micah Zenko and Sarah Kreps, *Limiting Armed Drone Proliferation* (New York: Council on Foreign Relations, 2014), 9.

35. Gordon Lubold, "Pentagon to Sharply Expand US Drone Flights over Next Four Years," *Wall Street Journal*, August 16, 2015.

36. Audrey Cronin, "Why Drones Fail," *Foreign Affairs*, July/August 2013.

37. Steve Coll, "The Unblinking Stare," *The New Yorker*, November 24, 2014.

38. Ibrahim Mothana, "How Drones Help Al qaeda," *New York Times*, June 13, 2012.

39. Gregory Johnsen, "How We Lost Yemen," *Foreign Policy*, August 6, 2013.

40. Dan Byman, "Why Drones Work," *Foreign Affairs*, July/August 2013.

41. C. Christine Fair, "For Now, Drones Are the Best Option," *New York Times*, January 29, 2013; Avery Plaw, "Drone Strikes Save Lives, American and Other," *New York Times*, November 14, 2012.

42. Patrick Johnston, "Does Decapitation Work? Assessing the Effectiveness of Leadership Targeting in Counterinsurgency Campaigns," *International Security*, Vol. 36, No. 4 (2012): 47–79.

43. Jenna Jordan, "When Heads Roll: Assessing the Effectiveness of Leadership Decapitation," *Security Studies*, 18 (2009): 719–755.

44. Micah Zenko, *Reforming US Drone Strike Policies* (New York: Council on Foreign Relations, 2013), 10.

45. Hakim Almasmari, Margaret Coker, and Siobhan Gorman, "Drone Kills Top Al Qaeda Figure," *Wall Street Journal*, October 1, 2011.

46. Eric Holder, "Letter to Patrick J. Leahy," May 22, 2013, available at http://www.justice.gov/slideshow/AG-letter-5-22-13.pdf.

47. Sabrina Siddiqui, "Obama 'Surprised,' 'Upset' When Anwar Al-Awlaki's Teenage Son Was Killed by U.S. Drone Strike," *Huffington Post*, April 23, 2013.

48. Craig Whitlock, "US Airstrike That Killed American Teen in Yemen Raises Legal, Ethical Questions," *Washington Post*, October 22, 2011.

49. Robbie Brown and Kim Severson, "2nd American in Strike Waged Qaeda Media War," *New York Times*, September 30, 2011.

50. Mark Schone and Matthew Cole, "American Jihadi Samir Khan Killed with Awlaki," *ABC News*, September 30, 2011.

51. Shashank Bengali, "Fourth US Drone Victim Influenced by Sept 11, War," *LA Times*, May 23, 2013.

52. "US Drone Strike Accidentally Killed 2 Hostages," *CNN*, April 23, 2015.

53. Greg Botelho and Ralph Ellis, "Adam Gadahn, American Mouthpiece of Al-Qaeda, Killed," *CNN*, April 23, 2015; Krishnadev Calamur, "US Operations Killed Two Hostages Held by Al-Qaeda, Including an American," *CNPR*, April 23, 2015.

54. Leon Panetta, *Worthy Fights: A Memoir of Leadership in War and Peace*, 387.

55. "Justice Department Memo Reveals Legal Case for Drone Strikes on Americans," *NBC News*, February 4, 2013.

56. Philip Ewing, "Rand Paul Pulls Plug on Nearly 13-Hour Filibuster on Drones," *Politico*, March 6, 2013.

57. Jim Michaels, "Rand Paul Filibustering Brennan Nomination to Lead CIA," *USA Today*, March 6, 2013.

58. Mark Mazzetti and Eric Schmitt, "US Militant, Hidden, Spurs Drone Debate," *New York Times*, February 28, 2014.

59. Charli Carpenter, "Parsing the Anti-drone Debate," *The Duck of Minerva*, November 12, 2013.

60. Quoted in Zenko and Kreps, *Limiting Armed Drone Proliferation*, 8.

61. Panetta, *Worthy Fights*, 388.

62. Greg Jaffe, "Former Defense Secretary Gates Warns against Lure of Drone Warfare," *Washington Post*, October 23, 2013.

63. Dave Majumdar, "Air Force Future UAV Roadmap Could Be Released as Early as Next Week," *US Naval Intelligence News*, November 13, 2013.

64. Aliya Sternstein, "Here's How You Hack a Military Drone," *Next Gov*, April 27, 2015.

65. "U-2 Has the Edge over Global Hawk," *Aviation Week and Space Technology*, March 10, 2014.

66. This includes a camera that has a wider panorama than the sensors that are currently on the Global Hawk as well as an airborne electro-optical sensor that can survey seven parts of the spectrum. See Seth Robson, "Air Force Plans Drone Upgrade to Replace U-2 Planes," *Stars and Stripes*, March 15, 2014.

67. Robson, "Air Force Plans Drone Upgrade."

68. Davis, "Armed and Dangerous?"

69. Anthea Elizabeth Roberts, "Traditional and Modern Approaches to Customary International Law: A Reconciliation," *American Journal of International Law*, Vol. 95, No. 4 (October 2001): 757–791.

70. John Brennan, "The Efficacy and Ethics of U.S. Counterterrorism Strategy," *Woodrow Wilson Center Transcript*, April 30, 2012.

71. Jane Mayer, "Torture and Obama's Drone Program," *The New Yorker*, February 15, 2013, available at http://www.newyorker.com/online/blogs/newsdesk/2013/02/torture-and-obamas-drone-program.html.

72. Department of Justice White Paper, available at https://lawfare.s3-us-west-2.amazonaws.com/staging/s3fs-public/uploads/2013/02/020413_DOJ_White_Paper.pdf.

73. O'Connell notes that states can also use force to suppress rebel uprisings or if a state has been invited to suppress an uprising. These latter two circumstances do not seem germane in terms of the use of drones. See Mary Ellen O'Connell, "Remarks: The Resort to Drones under International Law," *Denver Journal of International Law*, Vol. 585, No. 39 (2010–2011): 585–600.

74. James Cavallaro, Stephan Sonnenberg, and Sarah Knuckey, *Living Under Drones: Death, Injury, and Trauma to Civilians from US Drone Practices in Pakistan*. Russell Christopher, "Imminence in Justified Targeted Killing," in *Targeted Killing: Law and Morality in Asymmetrical Conflict*, Claire Finkelstein, Jens David Ohlin, and Andrew Altman, eds. (Oxford, UK: Oxford University Press, 2012), 253–284; 284.

75. Judith Gail Gardam, "Proportionality and Force in International Law," *American Journal of International Law*, Vol. 87, No. 3 (1993): 391–413.

76. "Article 57 Additional Protocol 1 to the Geneva Conventions," (1977), Part IV: Civilian Population.

77. "Article 57 Additional Protocol 1 to the Geneva Conventions" (1977). It should be noted that even though the United States has not ratified AP I, the principles embedded in it are generally considered customary law. Jean-Marie Henckaerts and Louise Doswald-Beck, *Customary International Humanitarian Law: Rules* (Cambridge, UK: Cambridge University Press), 51.

78. Additional Protocol I, 1977; Part IV: Civilian Population.

79. Max Boot, "The New American Way of War," *Foreign Affairs*, Vol. 82, No. 4 (2003): 41–58.

80. Sarah Kreps and John Kaag, "The Use of Unmanned Aerial Vehicles in Contemporary Conflict: A Legal and Ethical Analysis," *Polity*, Vol. 44 (2012): 260–285; 2.

81. Quoted in Scott Shane, "The Moral Case for Drones," *New York Times*, July 14, 2012.

82. Common Article 3 of the Geneva Conventions, available at http://www.icrc.org/ihl.nsf/WebART/375-590006.

83. ICRC, "Interpretive Guidance on the Notion of Direct Participation in Hostilities under IHL," *International Review of the Red Cross*, Vol. 90, No. 872 (Dec 2008): 991–1047.

84. William J. Fenrick, "The *Targeted Killings* Judgment and the Scope of Direct Participation in Hostilities," *Journal of International Criminal Law*, Vol. 5, No. 2 (2007): 332–338.

85. Jens David Ohlin, "Targeting Co-Belligerents," in *Targeted Killings: Law and Morality in an Asymmetrical World* (New York: Oxford University Press, 2012), 68.

86. "Attorney General Eric Holder Speaks at Northwestern University School of Law," *Department of Justice Transcript*, March 5, 2012.

87. "Remarks by the President at the National Defense University," Ft. McNair, May 23, 2013.

88. Bradley Jay Strawser, "Moral Predators: The Duty to Employ Uninhabited Aerial Vehicles," *Journal of Military Ethics*, Vol. 9, No. 4 (2010): 342–368.

89. John Kaag and Sarah Kreps, "The Moral Hazard of Drones," *New York Times*, July 22, 2012.

90. Kelley McMillan, "Ski Helmet Use Not Reducing Brain Injuries," *New York Times*, January 4, 2014.

91. Zenko and Kreps, *Limiting Armed Drone Proliferation*, 10.

92. Michael Walzer, "Targeted Killing and Drone Warfare," *Dissent*, January 11, 2013.

93. Special thanks to a former Air Force Predator pilot, December 22, 2014.

94. Dave Majumdar, "Exclusive: US Drone Fleet at 'Breaking Point,'" Air Force Says," *The Daily Beast*, January 4, 2015.

95. James Dao, "Drone Pilots Are Found to Get Stress Disorders as Much as Those in Combat Do," *New York Times*, February 22, 2013.

96. Author's interview with former Predator pilot, December 22, 2014.

97. Ibid.

98. Ernesto Londono, "Pentagon Cancels Divisive Distinguished Warfare Medal for Cyber Ops, Drone Warfare," *Washington Post*, April 15, 2013.

99. Jim Garamone, "Hagel Replaces Distinguished Warfare Medal with New Device," *American Forces Press Service*, April 15, 2013.

100. Dao, "Drone Pilots Are Found to Get Stress Disorders Much as Those in Combat Do," 2013.

101. Brian Fung, "The Army's Drone Pilots Aren't Being Trained because They're Too Busy Mowing Lawns," *Washington Post*, May 15, 2015.

102. Immanuel Kant, "Towards Perpetual Peace," in *The Basic Writings of Kant*, ed. Allen Wood (New York: Random House, 2001), 422.

103. Dan Reiter and Allan Stam, *Democracies at War* (Princeton, NJ: Princeton University Press, 2002).

104. John Kaag and Sarah Kreps, "Drones and Democratic Peace," *Brown Journal of World Affairs*, Vol. 19, No. 2 (Spring/Summer 2013): 1–13.

105. For comprehensive public opinion polls on Afghanistan, see http://www.gallup.com/poll/116233/afghanistan.aspx.

106. "US Supports Some Domestic Drone Use," Monmouth University poll, June 12, 2012.

107. Ryan Goodman, "Targeting Al-Shabaab's Godane Is Not the Same as Targeting Al-Shabaab," *Just Security*, September 2, 2014.

108. Charlie Savage and Mark Landler, "White House Defends Continuing US Role in Libya Operation," *New York Times*, June 15, 2011.

109. Harold Koh, "Obama's ISIL Legal Rollout: Bungled, Clearly. But Illegal? Really?" *Just Security*, September 29, 2014.

Chapter 3

1. General Accountability Office, 2012 report on the proliferation of UAVs. *Nonproliferation: Agencies Could Improve Information Sharing and End-Use Monitoring on Unmanned Aerial Vehicle Exports*, 2012.

2. Kelley Sayler, *A World of Proliferated Drones: A Technology Primer* (Washington, DC: Center for a New American Security, 2015), 17.

3. Davis et al., *Armed and Dangerous*.

4. Jefferson Morley, "Israel's Drone Dominance," *Salon*, May 15, 2012.

5. Defense Security Cooperation Agency, November 4, 2015, available at http://www.dsca.mil/major-arms-sales/italy-weaponization-mq-9s.

6. "Spain to Buy 4 US Surveillance Drones," *Defense News*, August 6, 2015.

7. Carlo Munoz, "Iraqi Military to Buy Unarmed Drones to Monitor Oil," *The Hill*, May 21, 2012.

8. Quoted in Zenko and Kreps, *Limiting Armed Drone Proliferation*, 16.

9. G. J. Harrison, *Unmanned Aircraft Systems (UAS): Manufacturing Trends*, US Congressional Research Service, 2012.

10. Scott Shane, "Coming Soon: The Drone Arms Race," *New York Times*, October 8, 2011.

11. Patrick Tucker, "Every Country Will Have Armed Drones within 10 Years," *Defense One*, May 6, 2014.

12. Daniel Byman, "Why Drones Work: The Case for Washington's Weapon of Choice," *Foreign Affairs*, July/August 2013.

13. The United States expects to have a drone bomber by the 2020s. See David Axe, "Russian Drones Lag US Models by 20 Years," *Wired*, August 6, 2012.

14. Graham Warwick and Larry Dickerson, "Shifting Growth," *Aviation Week*, 79.

15. "German Defense Minister Seeks Armed Drones for Military," *Deutsche Welle*, July 1, 2014.

16. "European Parliament Resolution on the Use of Armed Drones (2014/2567(RSP))," European Parliament, February 25, 2014.

17. "JFK on Nuclear Weapons and Non-proliferation," http://carnegieendowment.org/2003/11/17/jfk-on-nuclear-weapons-and-non-proliferation.

18. Craig Whitlock, "Close Encounters on Rise as Small Drones Gain in Popularity," *Washington Post*, June 23, 2014.

19. Steven Overly, "For the US Satellite Industry, Strict Export Controls Cost Market Share," *Washington Post*, March 27, 2011.

20. Christof Heyns, *Report of the Special Rapporteur on Extrajudicial, Summary or Arbitrary Executions*, 2014, 5.

21. Erik Pineda, "2 Signs Russia Remains Combat-Ready vs US, NATO: Increased Baltic Sea Incursions and Relentless Naval Build-Up," *International Business Times*, December 10, 2014.

22. "The Chinese Military's Response to Unannounced Drones: Blow 'Em Out of the Sky," *Wall Street Journal*, December 15, 2014.

23. Mehrdad Balali and Michelle Moghtader, "Iran Says It Shoots Down Israeli Spy Drone," *Reuters*, August 24, 2014.

24. Panetta, *Worthy Fights*, 435.

25. Robert Jervis, *Perception and Misperception in International Politics* (Princeton, NJ: Princeton University Press 1978), 29.

26. Ibid., 23.

27. Richard Whittle, "Turkey Boasts New Predator Drone Clone; Displayed at AUSA," *Breaking Defense*, October 15, 2014.

28. Mary Catherine O'Connor, "Here Come the Swarming Drones," *The Atlantic*, October 31, 2014.

29. E. Miasnikov, *Threat of Terrorism Using Unmanned Aerial Vehicles: Technical Aspects*, Center for Arms Control, Energy and Environmental Studies, 2014.

30. Kelley Sayler, *A World of Proliferated Drones*, 29.

31. Breanna Edwards, "Dianne Feinstein: Time to Set Drone Rules," *Politico*, March 7, 2013.

32. Van Jackson, "Kim Jong Un's Tin Can Air Force," *Foreign Policy*, November 12, 2014.

33. C. Muñoz, "Iran Claims Drones Gained Access to Secret Israeli Facilities," *The Hill*, October 29, 2012, available at https://thehill.com/policy/defense/264691-iran-claims-drones-gained-access-to-secret-israeli-facilities. See also M. Hoenig, *Hezbollah and the Use of Drones as a Weapon of Terrorism*, Federation of American Scientists, 2014.

34. Caroline Alexander and Gwen Ackerman, "Hamas Bragging Rights Grow with Drones Use against Israel," *Bloomberg*, July 16, 2014.

35. "Hamas Flexes Muscles with Gaza Drone Flight," *Agence France-Presse*, December 14, 2014.

36. Davis et al., *Armed and Dangerous*, 2014.

37. "New Imagery Details Indian Aura UCAV," *Aviation Week*, July 16, 2012.

38. Zenko and Kreps, *Limiting Armed Drone Proliferation*, 18.

39. "Study on the Development of a Framework for Improving End-Use and End-User Control Systems" (Geneva, Switzerland: UNODA Occasional Papers, 2011), 6.

40. Sydney Freedberg Jr., "Military 'Aggressively Working' to Ease Drone Sales Abroad," *Breaking Defense*, August 9, 2012.

41. In the notification to Congress, the Obama administration did not indicate that the United States would have to contend with the MTCR's strong presumption of denial for exports of the Global Hawk. See Jim Wolf, "US Moves to Sell Advanced Spy Drones to South Korea," *Reuters*, December 25, 2012; James Hardy, "Update: Singapore Airshow 2014: Northrop Grumman Hopeful of South Korean Global Hawk Deal Soon," *Jane's Defense Weekly*, February 11, 2014.

42. Allen Buchanan and Robert Keohane, "International Institutional Regulation of Lethal Drones," Princeton University, 2014.

43. Zenko and Kreps, *Limiting Armed Drone Proliferation*, 78.

44. Ben Emmerson, *Report of the Special Rapporteur on the Promotion and Protection of Human Rights and Fundamental Freedoms While Countering Terrorism*, 2014, available at http://www.lawfareblog.com/wp-content/uploads/2014/02/A-HRC-25-59.doc; 7–9.

45. Christof Heyns, *Report by the UN Special Rapporteur on Extrajudicial, Summary or Arbitrary Executions*, 2014, 23.

46. Zenko and Kreps, *Limiting Armed Drone Proliferation*, 25.

47. Ben Popper, "Homeland Security Is Testing Nightmare Scenarios Where Toy Drones Become Flying Bombs," *The Verge*, February 6, 2015.

48. Tessa Berenson, "Drone Carrying Meth Crashes Near Mexico Border," *Time*, January 22, 2015.

Chapter 4

1. "iRobot 510 PackBot," available at http://www.irobot.com/For-Defense-and-Security/Robots/510-PackBot.aspx#PublicSafety.

2. Tim Hornyak, "iRobot Military Bots to Patrol 2014 World Cup in Brazil," *CNET*, May 15, 2013.

3. Elisabeth Braw, "How Robot Dogs Are Changing the Face of Warfare," *Newsweek*, July 1, 2014.

4. TALON, by QinetiQ North America, available at https://www.qinetiq-na.com/products/unmanned-systems/talon/.

5. Paul McLeary, "US Army's Unmanned Ground Vehicle Research Creeps Along," *Defense News*, May 13, 2014.

6. "The Inside Story of the SWORDS Armed Robot 'Pullout' in Iraq: Update," *Popular Mechanics*, October 1, 2009.

7. Paul McLeary, "US Army's Unmanned Ground Vehicle Research Creeps Along," *Defense News*, May 13, 2014.

8. "Unmanned Ground Vehicle Market by Application," *Markets and Markets*, September 2014.

9. "Unmanned Ground Vehicles: Core Capabilities & Market Background" (2013), The Association for Unmanned Vehicle Systems International, available at http://higherlogicdownload.s3.amazonaws.com/AUVSI/f28f661a-e248-4687-b21d-34342433abdb/UploadedFiles/AUVSIUGVCoreCapabilitiesandMarketBackground08-08-13.pdf.

10. "Europe's Focus on Unmanned Network Centric Solutions to Boost the Unmanned Ground Vehicles Market, Says Frost and Sullivan," August 4, 2010, *Frost & Sullivan*, available at http://www.frost.com/prod/servlet/press-release.pag?docid=208494369.

11. Richard Tomkins, "Israel Defense Forces to Deploy More Unmanned Ground Vehicles," *UPI*, June 3, 2014.

12. http://www.idf.il/1283-17082-EN/Dover.aspx.

13. Walter Farah, "Unmanned Ground Vehicles, Guardium MK III," July 2, 2013, available at https://walterfarah.wordpress.com/tag/guardium/.

14. "The IDF's Latest Wizardry: Unmanned Ground Vehicles," IDF Spokesperson's Office, June 3, 2014.

15. David Hambling, "Russia Wants Autonomous Fighting Robots, and Lots of Them," *Popular Mechanics*, May 12, 2014.

16. Ibid.

17. Sushant Kulkarni, "Faster, Lighter, DRDO's Daksh Now Has CBRN Detection Mechanism," *The Indian Express*, September 26, 2015.

18. "PLA Working to Develop Unmanned Armored Vehicles," *China Daily USA*, July 23, 2014.

19. Jon Grevatt, "China Inaugurates UGV Facility," *HIS Jane's 360*, July 23, 2014.

20. Author's interview, E-7 soldier from the 82nd Airborne; January 14, 2015.

21. Dean Nelson, "Indian Soldier Beheaded by Pakistani Troops as Kashmir Dispute Escalates," *Telegraph*, January 8, 2013.

22. "UN Observers Claim to Have Witnessed Israeli Drones Prior to Golan Strike," *Jerusalem Post*, January 20, 2015.

23. Sally Cole, "Unmanned Underwater Vehicles Modernize US Navy's Sea-Mine-Hunting Capabilities," *Military Embedded Systems*, available at http://mil-embedded.com/articles/unmanned-navys-sea-mine-hunting-capabilities/.

24. Department of Defense Unmanned Undersea Vehicles information, available at www.dtic.mil/ndia/2005umv_auv/thursday/wood.pdf.

25. "US Moving Submersibles to Persian Gulf to Oppose Iran," *LA Times*, July 11, 2012.

26. Samuel Brannan, *Sustaining the US Lead in Unmanned Systems: Military and Homeland Considerations through 2025* (Washington, DC: CSIS 2014), 11.

27. "Spartan Unmanned Surface Vehicle Successful Live-Fire Tests," US Naval Sea Systems Command, May 11, 2005, available at http://www.defense-aerospace.com/articles-view/release/3/56957/spartan-unmanned-boat-in-live-fire-tests-(may-12).html.

28. "Spartan USVs for Singapore's Navy," *Defense Industry Daily*, May 18, 2005, available at http://www.defenseindustrydaily.com/spartan-usvs-for-singapores-navy-0540/.

29. Andrew Tarantola, "US Coasts Could be Guarded by Unmanned Drone Boats," *Gizmodo*, April 11, 2012.

30. Robert Brizzolara, "Surface Autonomy Is Heading for the Fleet," *Future Force*, March 28, 2014.

31. David Smalley, "The Future is Now: Navy's Autonomous Swarmboats can Overwhelm Adversaries," Office of Naval Research, available at http://www.onr.navy.mil/Media-Center/Press-Releases/2014/autonomous-swarm-boat-unmanned-caracas.aspx.

32. "Pioneer Short Range (SR) UAV," Federation of American Scientists, available at http://www.fas.org/irp/program/collect/pioneer.htm.

33. "In a First, Unmanned Navy Jet Lands on Aircraft Carrier," *NPR*, July 10, 2013.

34. Sam LaGrone, "Compromise Defense Bill Restricts Navy UCLASS Funds," *US Naval Intelligence News*, December 3, 2014.

35. "Israel Defense Forces to Develop Drone Submarines, Market Expected to Reach $2 Billion," *The Algemeiner*, October 17, 2013.

36. Henry Kenyon, "Israel Deploys Robot Guardians," *Signal*, March 2006.

37. Yuval Azulai, "Israel to Develop Unmanned Submarines," *Globes*, October 15, 2013.

38. Nick Hopkins, "Ministry of Defense Plans New Wave of Unmanned Marine Drones," *The Guardian*, August 2, 2012.

39. "Russian Navy Plans on Commissioning Undersea Reconnaissance Drone in 2 Years—Newspaper," *RT*, June 26, 2014.

40. Carl Schuster, "Drones Take South China Sea Plunge," *Asia Times*, August 29, 2012.

41. Manoj Das, "Navy Plans Unmanned Aircraft to Tackle Piracy," *India Times*, June 16, 2013. http://timesofindia.indiatimes.com/india/Navy-plans-unmanned-aircraft-to-tackle-piracy/articleshow/20609697.cms.

42. Manoj Das, "Navy Plans Unmanned Aircraft to Tackle Piracy," *The Times of India*, June 16, 2013.

43. Christopher Harress, "Sweden Confirms Secret Second Hunt for Another Russian Submarine," *International Business Times*, January 12, 2015.

44. Antoine Martin, "US Expands Use of Underwater Unmanned Vehicles," *National Defense Magazine*, April 2012.

45. Kelly Dickerson, "Underwater Drones Map Algae beneath Antarctic Ice," *Live Science*, January 13, 2015.

46. Julie Makinen, "Underwater Vehicle to Look for Malaysia Jet in Area 'New to Man,'" *LA Times*, April 13, 2014.

Chapter 5

1. Steve Dent, "What You Need to Know about Commercial Drones," *engadget*, June 13, 2014.

2. "How Many Drones Monitor US Borders?" *Christian Science Monitor*, available at http://www.csmonitor.com/Photo-Galleries/Infographics/The-future-of-drones-in-the-US#705889.

3. Craig Whitlock and Craig Timberg, "Border Patrol Drones Being Borrowed by Other Agencies More Often Than Previously Known," *The Washington Post*, January 14, 2014.

4. Jack Nicas, "Drone Patrols on US Border Ineffective, Report Finds," *Wall Street Journal*, January 6, 2015.

5. "Can Americans Challenge Evidence Collected by Drones?" *Christian Science Monitor*, April 19, 2014.

6. Ed Pilkington, "'We See Ourselves as the Vanguard': The Police Force Using Drones to Fight Crime," *The Guardian*, October 1, 2014.

7. James Wood, "City Rolls Out Drone Monitoring Program," *Meridian Booster*, March 31, 2015.

8. Melissa Pamer and Mark Mester, "LAPD's 2 Drones Will Remain Grounded during Policy Review, Police Commission Says amid Protest," *KTLA*, September 15, 2014.

9. Jonah Spangenthal-Lee, "SPD UAVs Leave Seattle to Try to Make It in Hollywood," *SPD Blotter*, June 2, 2014, available at http://spdblotter.seattle.gov/2014/06/02/spd-uavs-leave-seattle-to-try-to-make-it-in-hollywood/.

10. "US Approves More Commercial Drone Use as Congress Probes Risks," *Reuters*, December 10, 2014.

11. Chris Wickham, "Military Drones Zero In on a $400 Billion Civilian Market," *Reuters*, November 14, 2012.

12. "Press Release—FAA Grants Five More Commercial UAS Exemptions," available at http://www.faa.gov/news/press_releases/news_story.cfm?newsId=17934&cid=TW286.

13. W. J. Hennigan, "FAA Allows First Commercial Drone Flights over Land," *LA Times*, June 10, 2014.

14. Hallie Busta, "The FAA's Latest Drone-Use Approvals Include Construction Firms," *Architect*, December 10, 2014.

15. Clay Dillow, "Drones to Speed Up Construction Costs," *Fortune*, December 29, 2014.

16. Lizzie Schiffman Tufano, "Loop-Based Clayco Corp Gets OK to Use Drones," *DNA Info*, December 11, 2014.

17. *AUVSI Economic Report 2013*, 6.

18. Graham Warwick and Larry Dickerson, "Shifting Growth," *Aviation Week and Space Technology*, December 29, 2014–January 11, 2015, 79–81.

19. Chad Garland, "Drones May Provide Big Lift to Agriculture When FAA Allows Their Use," *LA Times*, September 13, 2014.

20. Miranda Green, "Unmanned Drones May Have Their Greatest Impact on Agriculture," *The Daily Beast*, March 26, 2013.

21. Letter requesting exemption for Amazon's testing of delivery drones, dated July 9, 2014, available at http://www.regulations.gov/contentStreamer?objectId=090000648179bc8f&disposition=attachment&contentType=pdf.

22. Alex Hern, "DHL Launches First Commercial Drone 'Parcelcopter' Delivery Service," *The Guardian*, September 25, 2014.

23. Colleen Taylor, "How Matternet Wants to Bring Drone Delivery to the People Who Need It Most," *Tech Crunch*, December 10, 2013.

24. Tekla Perry, "Matternet's Package Delivery Drones," *IEEE Spectrum Techwise Conversation*, December 19, 2013.

25. Ellen Gamerman, "Drones Invade Hollywood," *Wall Street Journal*, March 26, 2015.

26. "CNN Teams Up with the FAA for Reporter Drones," *The Hollywood Reporter*, January 12, 2015.

27. Dylan Byers, "CNN Strikes Drone Deal with FAA," *Politico*, January 12, 2015.

28. Eddie Pells, "Winter X Games to Use Drones to Capture Action on Snow," *ABC News*, January 20, 2015.

29. Linda Qiu, "Watch: Can Drones Help Save Wildlife around the World?" *National Geographic*, November 14, 2014.

30. Mark Stevenson, "Mexico to Use Drones to Protect Endangered Porpoise," *ABC News*, January 19, 2015.

31. "About wcUAVc," *Wildlife Conservation UAV Challenge*, available at http://www.wcuavc.com/#!leadership/cktc.

32. Patrick Tucker, "The Secret Weapon in the War on Poaching . . . and Terrorism," *Defense One*, April 28, 2014.

33. Matt McFarland, "American Red Cross Takes Serious Look at Using Drones for Disaster Relief, Holds Off for Now," *Washington Post*, April 21, 2015.

34. Lauren Pelley, "Drone Popularity Soaring This Holiday Season," *Toronto Star*, December 22, 2014.

35. This includes about 100 per week of the drones his company, 3D Robotics, makes.

36. This does not include other online drone enthusiast communities that exist, though DIYdrones.com appears to be the largest. See Chris Anderson, "How I Accidentally Kickstarted the Domestic Drone Boom," *Wired*, June 22, 2012.

37. Todd Bishop, "No Fad: Consumer Drones Will Become a $1 Billion Global Sector by 2018, Economist Says," *Geek World*, January 4, 2015.

38. Tracy Staedter, "Tasty Tech Eye Candy of the Week: Drones Attack," *Discovery News*, December 28, 2014.

39. Chris Anderson, "Why We Shouldn't Fear Personal Drones," *Time*, January 31, 2013.

40. Kate Murphy, "Things to Consider Before Buying That Drone," *New York Times*, December 6, 2014.

41. Author's interview with Ray Kelly, February 2014.

42. "Drones Nearly Collide with NYPD Helicopter, Two Arrested," *RT*, July 8, 2014.

43. Craig Whitlock, "Close Encounters on Rise as Small Drones Gain in Popularity," *Washington Post*, June 23, 2014.

44. Tara Patel, "Mystery Drones in France Expose Vulnerability of Nuclear Sites," *Bloomberg Businessweek*, November 4, 2014.

45. "Britain's Nuclear Plants 'Could be Attacked by Drones': Report," *The Hindu*, December 21, 2014.

46. Armin Rosen, "The Navy's New Drone-Killing Laser May Not Be as Impressive as It Seems," *Business Insider*, May 19, 2015.

47. Robot Dragonfly, Micro Aerial Vehicle, available at https://www.indiegogo.com/projects/robot-dragonfly-micro-aerial-vehicle.

48. Rand Paul, "Don't Let Drones Invade Our Privacy," *CNN*, June 15, 2012.

49. Letter from Rand Paul to Robert Mueller, June 20, 2013.

50. Catherine Crump, "What the FBI Needs to Tell Americans about Its Use of Drones," *American Civil Liberties Union*, July 26, 2013.

51. FBI Letter to Senator Rand Paul, July 19, 2013.

52. FBI Letter to Members Lofgren and Poe, July 19, 2013.

53. Richard Thompson II, *Drones in Domestic Surveillance Operations: Fourth Amendment Implications and Legislative Responses*, Congressional Research Service, April 3, 2013, 14.

54. Brendan Sasso, "Police Drones Prompt Privacy Concerns," *The Hill*, November 3, 2012.

55. John Villasenor, "Will 'Drones' Outflank the Fourth Amendment?" *Forbes*, September 20, 2012.

56. Ibid.

57. Andrew Couts, "Drones: 13 Things You Need to Know: Congress's New Report," *Digital Trends*, September 12, 2012.

58. Wells Bennett, "Civilian Drones, Privacy, and the Federal-State Balance," *Brookings Institution*, September 2014.

59. Joan Lowy, "AP-NCC Poll: A Third of the Public Fears Police Use of Drones for Surveillance Will Erode Their Privacy," *Associated Press*, September 27, 2012.

60. Rasmussen poll conducted October 24–25, 2013.

61. Emily Ekins, "Reason-Rupe December 2013 National Survey," December 13, 2013.

62. *Unmanned Aircraft and the Human Element: Public Perceptions and First Responder Concerns*, Institute for Homeland Security Solutions Research Brief, June 2013.

63. "Summary," in Richard Thompson II, *Drones in Domestic Surveillance Operations: Fourth Amendment Implications and Legislative Responses*, Washington, DC: Congressional Research Service, 2013.

64. Paul Hollis, "FAA Drone Ruling Said to Be Setback for Farmers," *Southeast Farm Press*, August 10, 2014.

65. Brian Naylor, "Sources: FAA May Require Licenses to Fly Commercial Drones," *NPR*, December 9, 2014.

66. Federal Aviation Administration, www.faa.gov/uas.

67. "Busting Myths about the FAA and Unmanned Aircraft," available at http://www.faa.gov/news/updates/?newsId=76240.

68. Sara Fischer, "FAA to Ramp Up Drone Education, Regulation," *CNN*, December 1, 2014.

69. Bart Alias, *Pilotless Drones*, CRS Report 2012, 8.

70. Ibid.

71. Keith Laing, "FAA Sets Up Final Drone Testing Site," *The Hill*, August 13, 2014.

72. Jordan Golson, "Rural Pilots Won't Be Happy about the FAA's New Drone Rules," *Wired*, November 26, 2014.

73. Justin Bachman, "Not an Airplane Pilot? You Won't Be Flying Commercial Drones," *Bloomberg Businessweek*, November 28, 2014.

74. *The Economic Impact of Unmanned Aircraft Systems Integration in the United States*, Association for Unmanned Vehicle Systems International, March 2013.

75. Jack Nicas and Andy Pasztor, "Drone Flights Face FAA Hit," *Wall Street Journal*, November 24, 2014.

76. "FAA 'Hundreds of Cases' of Operating Drones 'Carelessly' & 'Recklessly,'" *CNN*, November 30, 2014.

77. Todd Bishop, "FAA Looking into Picture Taken by Drone above Space Needle," *GeekWire*, December 10, 2014.

78. Michael Berry and Nabiha Syed, "State Legislation Governing Private Drone Use," *Washington Post*, September 25, 2014.

79. Allie Bohm, "The Year of the Drone: An Analysis of State Legislation Passed This Year," *ACLU*, November 7, 2013.

80. Allie Bohm, "The First State Laws on Drones," *ACLU*, April 15, 2013.

81. Joe Wolverton II, "Gov Rick Scott Signs Florida Drone Regulation Bill," *The New American*, April 25, 2013.

82. Don Soloman, "Texas's Drone Law Is Pretty Much the Opposite of Every Other State's Drone Law," *Texas Monthly*, September 17, 2013.

83. Christina Mulligan, "Georgia Prepares for the Drone Industry," *InterDrone*, May 27, 2015, available at http://www.interdrone.com/news/georgia-prepares-for-the-drone-industry.

84. Allie Bohm, "The Year of the Drone: An Analysis of State Legislation Passed This Year," *American Civil Liberties Union*, November 7, 2013.

85. Thomas Claburn, "Google Tests Delivery Drones," *Information Week*, September 2, 2014.

86. UAV Global Unmanned Systems and Manufacturers, available at http://www.uavglobal.com/list-of-manufacturers/.

87. Clay Dillow, "Despite FAA Dithering, a Drone Economy Sprouts on the Farm," *Fortune*, September 16, 2014.

88. *The Economic Impact of Unmanned Aircraft Systems Integration in the United States*, 5.

89. Transport Canada, "Flying an Unmanned Aircraft Recreationally," available at http://www.tc.gc.ca/eng/civilaviation/standards/general-recavi-uav-2265.htm?WT.mc_id=21zwi.

90. Jim Bronskill, "Study Warns That Unmanned Drones over Canada Could Be 'Intrusive,'" *CTV News*, November 12, 2013.

91. "Permission and Safety Requirements," available at http://www.tc.gc.ca/eng/civilaviation/standards/standards-4179.html.

92. Safety requirements available at http://wwwapps.tc.gc.ca/Saf-Sec-Sur/2/NPA-APM/doc.aspx?id=10293.

93. Andrew Trotman, "Hearing a Buzzing Noise? It Could Be Amazon Testing Its Drones," *Telegraph*, November 13, 2014.

94. *SUA Operators*. Rep. UK CAA, available at http://www.caa.co.uk/docs/1995/Dec2014%20Report%20UAVcurrentDates.pdf.

95. Charles Arthur, "Amazon Seeks US Permission to Test Prime Air Delivery Drones," *The Guardian*, July 11, 2014.

96. Andy Pasztor, "U.S., Europe Differ on Approach to Commercial Drones," *The Wall Street Journal*, June 18, 2014.

97. Graham Warwick and Larry Dickerson, "Shifting Growth," *Aviation Week and Space Technology*, December 29, 2014–January 11, 2015.

98. Connor Adams Sheets, "China Beat Amazon Prime Air to the Commercial Drone Delivery Market," *International Business Times*, December 2, 2013.

99. "Panique en China a cause d'un drone," *Le Figaro*, October 23, 2014.

100. Adrian Wan, "Little Airspace Free for Commercial Drones in China," *South China Morning Post*, August 7, 2013.

101. Jeremy Blum, "Chinese Delivery Company Develops Drones Which Can Fly Packages to Your Doorstep," *South China Morning Post*, December 24, 2014.

102. Emile Orzea, "China's UAS Regulation," *Small UAS News*, November 4, 2014.

103. Crispin Andrews, "Wildlife Monitoring: Should UAV Drones Be Banned?" *Engineering and Technology Magazine*, July 14, 2014.

104. Caitlin Kauffman, "Green Life: Poachers v. Drones: The Next Frontier," *Sierra*, May/June 2014.
105. Letter from Jeff Bezos to FAA Administrator Michael Huerta, July 9, 2014.
106. Krithika Krishnamurthy, "India to Be Launch Pad for Amazon's Plan to Deliver Packages Using Drones; Deliveries May Start by Diwali," *India Times*, August 20, 2014.
107. Tim Bradshaw, "Google Tests Drone Deliveries in Australia," *Financial Times*, August 29, 2014.
108. Jack Stewart, "Google Tests Drone Deliveries in Project Wing Trials," *BBC*, August 28, 2014.
109. Thomas Claburn, "Google Tests Delivery Drones," *Information Week*, September 2, 2014.
110. Ben Vogel, "EASA Weighs Up Civil Certification of Airbus UAV," *HIS Jane's Airport Review*, October 14, 2014.
111. Pasztor, "US, Europe Differ on Approach to Commercial Drones."

Chapter 6

1. Meghan Neal, "The Pentagon's Vision for the Future of Military Drones," *Vice*, December 28, 2013.
2. Zoe Kleinman, "CES 2015: Why the Future of Drones Is Up in the Air," *BBC*, January 8, 2015.
3. FAA Forecast 201048.
4. Christopher Harress, "Here's What the Future of Insect and Nano Drones Looks Like," *Investor Business Times*, January 9, 2014.
5. Air Force Bugbot Nano Drone Laboratory, by the Air Force Research Laboratory, April 11, 2013, available at https://www.youtube.com/watch?v=z78mgfKprdg.
6. Air Force Research Lab, April 11, 2013.
7. Zach Honig, "T-Hawk UAV Enters Fukushima Danger Zone, Returns with Video," *engadget*, April 21, 2011.
8. Darren Quick, "TechJect's Dragonfly Micro UAV Flies Like a Bird and Hovers Like an Insect," *gizmag*, November 7, 2012.
9. Julie Watson, "On the Wings of Technology: Hummingbird Drones," *NBC News*, February 28, 2011.
10. Andrew Tarantola, "Black Hornet: The $195,000 Spy Plane That Fits in the Palm of Your Hand," *Gizmodo*, February 6, 2013.
11. The author's October 15, 2014, visit to the lab and interview with Sujata Bhatia, lecturer on Biomedical Engineering at Harvard University, revealed the complexity of this microbiotics technology.

12. Adam Piore, "Rise of the Insect Drones," *Popular Science*, January 29, 2014.

13. Darlene Storm, "Google's Eric Schmidt Worried about Privacy from Civilian Nano Drones," *Computer World*, April 16, 2013.

14. James Ball, "Drones Should Be Banned from Private Use, Says Google's Eric Schmidt," *The Guardian*, April 20, 2013.

15. Douglas Ernst, "Nano Drone a Kickstarters Success; Personal Paparazzi Devices Ship in 2015," *The Washington Times*, December 9, 2014.

16. Mark Thompson, "Air Force Argument for New Bomber Bombs, Top General Says," *Time*, July 14, 2011.

17. DOD, Unmanned Systems Integrated Roadmap FY2009–2034 (Washington, DC: GPO, April 20, 2009), available at www.dtic.mil/dtic/tr/fulltext/u2/a522247.pdf, 27.

18. DoD Roadmap 2009, 10.

19. Kreps and Kaag, "UAV Analysis," 25.

20. Ronald Arkin and Patrick Ulam, "An Ethical Adapter: Behavioral Modification Derived from Moral Emotions," *IEEE* Technical Report GIT-GVU-09-04, 2009, available at http://www.cc.gatech.edu/ai/robot-lab/online-publications/ArkinUlamTechReport2009.pdf.

21. Ronald Arkin, *Governing Lethal Behavior in Autonomous Robots*, Chapman and Hall, 2009.

22. Reaching Critical Will, Fully Autonomous Weapons, available at http://www.reachingcriticalwill.org/resources/fact-sheets/critical-issues/7972-fully-autonomous-weapons.

23. "UN: 'Killer Robot' Talks Go Forward, Slowly," November 14, 2014, available at http://www.hrw.org/news/2014/11/14/un-killer-robot-talks-go-forward-slowly.

24. Tom Risen, "Musk, Hawking Call to Ban Robots That Could Kill You All by Themselves," *US News*, July 27, 2015.

25. Michael Horowitz and Paul Scharre, "Do Killer Robots Save Lives," *Politico*, November 19, 2014.

26. Robin Marantz Henig, "Death by Robot," *New York Times*, January 9, 2015.

27. Stu Robarts, "Google X Takes Wraps off Project Developing Autonomous Delivery Drones," *Giz Mag*, August 28, 2014.

28. Ryan Gajewski, "'Back to the Future II': 8 Predictions It Got Wrong about 2015," *The Hollywood Reporter*, January 5, 2015.

29. Roger Ebert, "Stealth," July 27, 2005, available at www.rogerebert.com/reviews/stealth-2005.

30. Heather Kelly, "Beer-Delivery Drone Grounded by FAA," *CNN*, February 3, 2014.

31. Fareed Zakaria, "American Innovation Is in Trouble," *Washington Post*, January 1, 2014.

32. Nick Bilton and John Markoff, "A Hardware Renaissance in Silicon Valley," *New York Times*, August 25, 2012.

33. Hiroko Tabuchi, "Venture Capitalists Return to Backing Science Start-Ups," *New York Times*, October 12, 2014.

34. Marcus Wohlsen, "The Ex-Googlers Building Drones That Anybody Can Pilot with a Phone," *Wired*, January 15, 2015.

35. Ben Popper, "A Tiny Startup Has Made Big Strides in Creating Self-Navigating Drones," *The Verge*, January 15, 2015.

36. Ibid.

37. Kevin Poulsen, "Why the US Government Is Terrified of Hobbyist Drones," *Wired*, February 5, 2015.

38. Gregory McNeal, "FAA's Proposed Drone Rules May Include Toy Drones," *Forbes*, January 29, 2015.

39. Alwyn Scott, "Americans OK with Police Drones—Private Ownership, Not So Much: Poll," *Reuters*, February 5, 2015.

40. Kelsey Atherton, "Ban Drones from Your Airspace with NoFlyZone," *Popular Science*, February 12, 2015.

41. Jackie Wattles, "Jeff Bezos: Amazon Drones Will Be as Common as Seeing a Mail Truck." *CNN*, August 16, 2015.

INDEX